FOR THOSE WHO SEEK
SACRED TRUTHS

IFTT PRESS

MINDFULNESS & MYSTICISM

Connecting Present Moment Awareness with Higher States of Consciousness

ORA NADRICH

MINDFULNESS & MYSTICISM
Ora Nadrich

Foreword by

His Holiness The 14th Dalai Lama

Published by:

IFTT Press

California, USA

Cover & Interior Design: Dmitriy Khanzhin

A CIP record for this book is available from the Library of Congress Cataloging-in-Publication Data

Library of Congress Control Number: 2021903760

ISBN: 978-0-578-98133-8

Printed in USA

" The most beautiful and profound emotion we can experience is the sensation of the mystical. He to whom this emotion is a stranger, who can no longer wonder and stand rapt in awe, is as good as dead. To know that what is impenetrable to us really exists, manifesting itself as the highest wisdom and the most radiant beauty, which our dull faculties can comprehend only in their primitive forms – this knowledge, this feeling, is at the center of true religion. "

— ALBERT EINSTEIN

TESTIMONIALS

"Mindfulness and Mysticism is both deeply mysterious and eminently practical. At a time when chaos in our culture is staggeringly upsetting, when millions are sensing there must be something 'more' but have no idea what it is, a book like this paves a path beyond confusion. It speaks to the mind as well as to the heart, both explaining the mystical and leading us into it. Ora Nadrich provides a traveler's companion from the delusional maze of a desacralized world, to the calm and inner peace that mindfulness can offer."

- MARIANNE WILLIAMSON
Presidential Candidate, Author

"There is nothing better than to read about the mind and states of consciousness than when written from a personal experience and understanding. Then, you can really understand your own experience more profoundly and only then any tools offered will do their alchemy. Ora's book is exactly that. It helped me reorganize my 'inner library' in a very useful way."

- DR. ALEJANDRO JUNGER

Author of Clean – The Revolutionary Program to Restore the Body's Natural Ability to Heal Itself

"Ora Nadrich has done a masterful job at bringing the practice of Mindfulness into the real world where you and I live that is undeniably user-friendly. She makes it clear that we don't 'have to be mystics' to have a deep, authentic connection to the present moment—while at the same time showing that, in truth, we already are mystics in training. That is the reason you have chosen to read this book; something within you is divinely stirring. The awakening to this truth comes to each of us when we are willing to mindfully step into the present moment with absolutely no hidden agenda—wherein the mystery of a mystical life awaits our arrival. You have chosen the right book, and Ora is the perfect guide. Consciousness always prevails! Trust her. Follow her lead because she knows the way well—the journey to the place you never really left: your oneness with the Beloved. What's not mystical about that?"

- DR. DENNIS MERRITT JONES

Award winning author of, The Art of Abundance - Ten Rules for a Prosperous Life, The Art of Uncertainty - How to Live In the Mystery of Life and Love It, and Your (Re)Defining Moments - Becoming Who You Were Born to Be

"Mindfulness and Mysticism is a beautifully written map to assist one's soul on the journey of awakening, self-discovery, and mystical illumination. With Mindfulness as the ever-present and guiding thread, the greater tapestry is becoming more present, mindful, and self-aware. The reader embarks upon the path of mystical self-transformation and divine inspiration to awaken to one's highest infinite potential. Ora Nadrich's book is a wonderful contribution for one's soul, and offers the reader a better understanding of how being in the present moment can raise our states of consciousness so that awakening and self-realization can be realized."

- RONALD A. ALEXANDER, PH.D

Author of Wise Mind, Open Mind

"A great Mindfulness book to help people through difficult times and help them enjoy the joyous times."

- LORIN ROCHE

Author of The Radiance Sutras, Meditation Made Easy

CONTENTS

FOREWORD BY
His Holiness The 14ᵗʰ Dalai Lama

When we encounter problems in life, the practice of mindfulness—being mentally aware—helps us gain a more realistic perspective on our situation and on what might be causing us difficulty. As we become more accustomed to this practice, we will see that our mind can be trained and that our negative thoughts and feelings can be transformed into more positive states of mind, thereby weakening the influence of negative emotions. Our ensuing peace of mind will enable us to be positive in life.

It is my firm belief that there is no better purpose in life than to benefit others. Meditation has different levels, perspectives and approaches. Ultimately, all should contribute to the wellbeing of others.

I hope that readers of Ora Nadrich's book, Mindfulness and Mysticism, will discover the techniques by which they can cultivate peace of mind and thereby more effectively take care or help our fellow brothers and sisters.

14

INTRODUCTION

*"Inability to accept the mystic experience
is more than an intellectual handicap."*

—ALAN WATTS

Years ago, I went to a therapist and tried to describe a very euphoric feeling I was experiencing but was having a hard time putting into words. The best way I could convey it was to say, "It's like feeling blissful on heroin."

I have never tried heroin, but it seemed like the perfect description because that's exactly what heroin produces, a feeling of euphoria.

I assume that when people try this highly addictive and extremely dangerous drug, it's because that's what they want to experience—a heightened state of bliss or elation. The reason for that, most often, is because they don't want to feel the pain or emptiness they have within themselves.

I wasn't trying to mask anything or escape from my feelings. I simply felt unexpected waves of ecstasy, which

15

is defined as "involving an experience of mystic self-tran-
scendence." It was rather mysterious to me and the therapist as to how I could experience this intense feeling of
euphoria without taking anything, but I guess if you go by
this anonymous quote, "Don't spend your life getting high
on drugs, get high on life," I was getting high on life.

But was life getting me high, or was it the chemicals
in my brain—such as Dopamine, a neurotransmitter that
makes us feel good and is considered part of the brain's
"reward system"—that were making me feel euphoric?

If our brain is able to reward us by releasing pleasur-
able, even ecstasy-like chemicals, why wouldn't we want to
delve deeper into its natural ability to produce it whenever we feel like it, or especially when we need it?

I believe we can. The chemicals in our brain read like
a medicine cabinet of opioids, which are drugs that act on
the nervous system to relieve pain. We have an assortment
of "feel- good" chemicals like Dopamine, which increases
focus, arousal, and pleasure; Norepinephrine, which increases adrenaline and awareness; Oxytocin, which creates
a feeling of deep connection, and a similar euphoria we
experience when we fall in love; Serotonin, which increases calmness and relaxation; and Prolactin, which also
produces a feeling of euphoria and can create a sense of
"oneness," which many have described as "mystical."

So, what is the mystical? Is it something we can only
experience when we're connecting to something like

religion, and tapping into the divine through worship? Or is it experienced by following a spiritual practice or discipline? Those are certainly two ways to have mystical experiences, but if we can have them, what that tells us is that we are capable of connecting to something that feels powerful, sacred, and even holy. And if we're not accessing it through us, and stimulating brain chemicals that can create a feeling of oneness, where do we think it's coming from?

We look at a sunset and are touched and moved by its beauty, but we are having the experience, the sun isn't making us have it. In essence, what I am saying is that we are experiencing the high and having the mystical experience. Things outside of ourselves can trigger the chemicals that trigger neurotransmitters, which make us feel elated or euphoric. But if we keep looking for bliss or ecstasy outside of ourselves, the mystical experience will remain a mystery, and the "high" will be something we believe can only be experienced through drugs, alcohol, and other stimulants, and not in our own brains without them.

Mindfulness, which is a mental state of being conscious and aware of everything around us, can also stimulate chemicals in our brain, depending on how conscious and aware we are in any given moment. The more we develop "present moment awareness," which Mindfulness is, the more we can trigger neurotransmitters consciously, or deliberately, which can make us feel high. The next thing you know, you're having a mystical experience watching a sunset, or seeing a star shoot across the night sky, or looking into a lover's eyes. Basically, everything can be a mystical experience if we're connecting to the "radiant beauty" of it, as Einstein said. But we must be fully present for that to happen, and allow our senses to be open and heightened so we can experience the mystical, which, as I said, can make us feel elated or high.

As the poet and Sufi mystic Rumi said, "I looked in temples, churches and mosques. But I found the divine in my heart." Do we feel we can only honor the divine outside of ourselves? Can we not accept that it lives within us, too? There is nothing wrong with worshipping the divine as something or someone outside of ourselves, but they, or "it," is a manifestation of us. When we feel a deep bliss or euphoria when we behold an image of a God or deity, or feel their essence in our heart, we are connecting to the mystical, the oneness, the exaltation that can make us feel so high, there is no drug or stimulant that can match it.

Whether you believe in a divine power outside of yourself, and worship it in a temple, church, mosque, or nowhere other than in your heart, you can experience mysticism, which is an altered state of consciousness that doesn't have to be esoteric, or only understood by those with specialized knowledge. Each of us can experience a mystical state of consciousness by being fully present and aware. If we think of ourselves as divine beings, which we are, and regard our body as a vessel to imbibe the mystical experience, we can experience a feeling of oneness created or enhanced by the chemicals in our brain, and consider the mystical realm as a normal reality in which to be. But instead, mysticism has been defined as "a belief without sound basis" or a "belief characterized by self-delusion or dreamy confusion of thought."

Evelyn Underhill, a poet and writer of Christian mysticism, describes it as the "Art of union with reality," and that reality can be filled with spiritual truths, which can create feelings of bliss and euphoria. So, what's delusional about that?

What is delusional is believing that the only way we can experience bliss and euphoria is through drugs, alcohol, or even the over use of our smart phones, which stimulates chemicals in the brain like dopamine. There's no wonder we can't stay off our devices when we are so used to the instant reward we get from successful social interactions. But the flip side of that is increased levels of anxiety and depression caused by the very thing we seek pleasure from when we can't disconnect from our devices in a healthy way.

Whatever it is we seek pleasure from, relying on external things to give us the high or a feeling of euphoria, we run the risk of deluding ourselves that we're in control when we're not. The opioid crisis is a perfect example of how out of control millions of people are over managing their dependency on feeling high, or numbing themselves from feeling anything uncomfortable.

What we're witnessing is tragic. The opioid crisis is being called the "most perilous drug crisis ever," taking the lives of approximately 91 people every day. The over-prescribing of opioids for people experiencing pain, some of it very moderate and manageable, and some which may have its bases in emotion, is completely out of control. Even with a warning that these drugs can kill you, once someone is dependent on them for numbing or ameliorating their pain, the risk of death is a price they are willing to pay so they can have temporary relief from their suffering.

This is not to say that pain can't be extremely difficult to endure, or even debilitating, and some people don't know of any way to stop their pain other than taking opioids. When prescribed safely, they can be used for the temporary relief of pain following something like surgery, or an injury. But once this mass addiction turns epidemic, which it has, and a genuine crisis exists, which it does, we know there is something much deeper that needs to be addressed. It has been terribly unfortunate that so many people have died, and continue to die, from overdosing. These highly addictive and dangerous drugs are not just being used by people who genuinely need proper medical treatment for physical pain, but by millions of people who are so stressed, or in such emotional anguish and turmoil, that they are using them to numb themselves completely, and there are far too many doctors prescribing opioids irresponsibly without warning of their extreme dangers.

Sadly, we have not been educated enough on how to use our own body's natural resources and healing abilities to work through our pain and suffering. We have not been taught early on such valuable and helpful tools as Mindfulness or meditation, which are known to reduce stress and anxiety, and are fortunately being practiced by many people to manage their pain and stress, including war veterans afflicted with PTSD, with very positive results. Until we stop looking outside of ourselves for answers, and as long as we keep avoiding the pain and suffering we will inevitably experience as human beings, we will continue to seek quick fixes to anesthetize ourselves from feeling anything. More and more people will fall into the downward spiral of addiction.

So, what is it that we are numbing ourselves from, and why so much drug and alcohol use? If our own brains can manufacture chemicals that can literally produce the type of endorphins that make us feel as good, or as high as a drug or alcohol can, why in the world aren't we looking within for the very gifts, remedies and even cures for what ails us? We have the answers, we just aren't asking ourselves the right questions.

"Insanity is doing the same thing over and over again

and expecting different results." This quote by Einstein, and also used in Al-Anon, a support group for loved ones of alcoholics, pretty much explains how we can foolishly repeat self-defeating patterns out of ignorance, rather than raising our awareness about how best to fix problems so that better results can be realized.

Don't we want better results? Aren't we ready to stop doing the same things over and over again, but instead try doing things differently, and maybe that means living our lives more mindfully and in tune with the "mystical"? By doing this, we may find the moments of our lives more magical, and rich with meaning, and only then can we truly experience less pain and more joy—even elation or euphoria.

Buddha told us there was suffering, and he was quite right, so what do we want to do about it? Stay dependent on drugs and alcohol, and use our devices to escape our pain, or bravely move through it and get on the other side of suffering where bliss can be its reward. And that reward comes from our brain releasing a plethora of chemicals that can make us feel so much better, even high.

It's true. Who needs to be dependent on drugs, or anything we feel we need to elevate us, when we can "get high on life"? If you're someone who likes your recreational drugs or alcohol and feels it increases, enhances, or adds bliss or euphoria to your life, I would suggest giving your brain chemicals a chance to show you what they can do without the use or help of anything that alters your mood. Instead, realize bliss, euphoria, and even higher states of consciousness by connecting to the great mystery that awaits you.

CHAPTER 1

BEHOLD MINDFULNESS

*With Mindfulness, you can establish yourself in the
present in order to touch the wonders of life that are
available in that moment.*

— THICH NHAT HAHN

*The moment one gives close attention to anything, even
a blade of grass, it becomes a mysterious,
awesome, incredibly magnificent world in itself.*

— HENRY MILLER

The living moment is everything.

— D.H. LAWRENCE

So, you think you're present. You have shown up in this moment. You are awake and aware. You are accepting and non-judgmental. You have no interest in your past. You could care less about the future. Is that correct?

We don't usually come to the present moment free of thoughts and concerns. And we don't travel light. As a matter of fact, we pack more than we need no matter where we go, and I'm talking about mental baggage. To show up somewhere with just you, and nothing else, is not easy to do. The reason for this is the "you," the "self," the person that we truly are, is not fully known to us, so how can we be fully present in the moment without knowing who we really are in it? Yes, we know ourselves, but that knowing is mostly based on our identity and what we do, or how we feel about ourselves in any given moment. And that changes because we change. We are constantly changing, but if we know that change is constant, and keep our awareness sharp about the impermanence of this life, then what remains constant is the "knowing," the "accepting" of change, and not being attached to what we think or believe will keep things permanent, which is nothing more than an illusion. And we like illusions, don't we? We like illusions because they can support what we need to believe in the moment to make it more acceptable to us, but it's still an illusion. We need what's real to keep us connected to reality as awake and aware as possible.

Practicing Mindfulness not only keeps us awake but also keeps us aware of the impermanence of life; therefore, we have a greater appreciation of it. We care. Life matters. The moments of our lives matter. We don't want to waste them. Not a single one. But we will because sometimes we can't help it. We get so involved in life, and distracted, and busy. So busy that we become too busy to stop. We can't stop being busy in the moment. We just can't unless we choose to stop and do things like meditate, and even in meditation our mind can remain active.

Mindfulness helps us, and we need it. We must not be so arrogant to think we can stay present and alert in every moment. We can't. Sometimes we can, if we really make a concerted effort to be present, but for the most part it's challenging. We are, as philosopher Pierre Teilhard de Chardin said, "Spiritual beings having a human experience." It's complicated. Being human is not simple or easy, and it challenges us daily to show up for life, or at least, *wanting* to show up for life. Many people don't even want to do that because life is too hard, painful, and even unbearable. It's just too much all the time. So, we escape the moments. We don't want them. We want them to go away. We want them to stop reminding us of how difficult life is, and they do, again and again.

What can we do with such a difficult life? What can we do with so much of our pain and suffering? Escape? Check out? Die? That's what millions of people do. They escape, either through drugs and alcohol, the overuse and dependency of their devices, or even choose to die through suicide when they can't take it anymore. They want out. And they want out desperately. How can you explain to someone who doesn't want to be here that this is heaven on earth? Yes, it can be hellish, but that can be overcome if we change the way we look at all of this, and Mindfulness helps us look at life differently. More heaven, and a lot less hell.

Here's how: Stand in front of the mirror and look at yourself. What do you see? Did you immediately judge yourself? Did you immediately criticize yourself? Did you immediately tell yourself that you're unattractive, or over-weight, or unlovable, or unworthy? Or did you look deep into your eyes and get lost? Look into those eyes of yours. Let them invite you in where you can meet yourself. Go ahead. Don't be afraid to go deeper into you. You have nothing to be afraid of. You just think that you do, and that is part of the problem, what we think. We think our-selves right out of the moment by telling ourselves how inadequate we are in it. This mind of ours never stops. Thousands and thousands of thoughts are going through our minds daily, and we do very little to regulate its activity. That's like allowing thousands of ants to traipse through your house without doing something about it, and we know how insidious ants can be. You look away, and the next thing you know, they've multiplied in droves.

Being present means we not only see the ants but we also mindfully take care of the problem. And, if the problem keeps recurring, which an ant problem most certainly can, we become even more mindful of what can solve that problem in the best way possible. And we do it with a very clear mind. You have a problem, and you take care of it with a clear-thinking mind. This is a mind that is uncluttered, unfettered, one that doesn't get lost in distraction or in thinking about something that happened yesterday, or worrying about what's going to happen next. You don't want to take care of an ant problem by wishing they weren't there or by worrying about more ants coming into your home. That's a complete waste of time.

I use the ant analogy because it shows where our mind can go, and how prone it is to wanting to go out of the moment. You can't go out of the moment if you have an infestation of ants in your home. You need to stay right there and fix it.

Mindfulness helps us stay right there, even when it's uncomfortable staying right there, and this is something very important for us to learn. We must discipline our mind to be present, aware, and focused, even when we would rather do anything but that. You see, we don't want to "go gentle into that good night," a line from a Dylan Thomas poem written for his dying father. We would rather "rage, rage against the dying of the light," fighting the pain and horrors of life, which is understandable. Fighting is good, but fight for life while you're living it, not just when your life is about to end. Stand up to the moments that are difficult and face them with total awareness. Be present with your pain, and be willing to feel it, *really feel it.* Yes, it can be very uncomfortable, but if you quickly try to numb yourself from it, then you are choosing to be in the moment half-asleep, and what kind of way is that to go through life?

Mindfulness is here for you, but you must use it, or it remains a valuable quality wasted. It will help you when you are sad or feeling hopeless by making you more aware of what's troubling you so you can know what to do about it. It's like it stops time and sits patiently with you, as if holding your hand and saying, "It's okay. You can be with what you're feeling, and take as much time as you need to work through it with compassion for yourself."

You see, Mindfulness is being in a state of total awareness of the contents of our minds, which makes us more conscious of what we're thinking and feeling. And, by being in this state of complete awareness, we can remain observant of our thoughts and feelings with acceptance and non-judgment because we have a heightened awareness of what is occurring in our minds. This is when we are in a pure state of mind, and it is in this state when you can guide yourself wisely, pointing yourself in the right direction instead of one that can be hurtful or harmful to you. This state of complete awareness that Mindfulness puts you in won't let you escape or choose something bad or unwise because you will be conscious of the choices you are making, and you will want to make the best ones. But, if you don't, that means you weren't letting Mindfulness do what it does so well—keep you present with total awareness.

Think of Mindfulness as an innate superpower. It's like having metacognition, which means you have a heightened awareness of what you're thinking in the moment, as well as a heightened awareness of your understanding of what you're thinking, and why. In essence, it means you are using "higher-order thinking skills" when you actively practice Mindfulness, and it can be powerful for sure. I consider it my North Star, always pointing me in the right direction. Do you know you have this type of power? You definitely have it. We all do, but maybe you haven't used it or relied on it as much as you can. When you do use it, it strengthens, and the more you use it, the more you get to take full advantage of the abundant, even "mystical" and transcendent gifts it can bring into your life.

Mindfulness, when practiced consistently, can feel like your awareness is so laser sharp that you can see things beyond what's on the surface. Are you aware like that? Most people aren't, but they can be if they decide to be more present. The more present you are, the more aware you are; and the more aware you are, the more present you are. It keeps evolving from there. Maybe you're not as aware as you'd like to be, so let me help you heighten your awareness a little more.

Look at your hands. What do you see? I don't mean *just* your hands, I mean everything *about* your hands. The color of your skin, the texture, the lines, the freckles or age spots, even your nails (they are part of your hands). Can you look at them without judging the way they look? Remember, Mindfulness is being in the present moment with "acceptance" and "non-judgment." Not so easy to do, right? Can you look at them as if you're seeing them for the first time? Can you look at them with curiosity and appreciation? Can you look at them with gratitude? Without them you couldn't eat, or get dressed, or touch yourself or someone else, or put on your make-up, or play sports, or an instrument, or drive a car, or wash your body, or open a window or a door, or walk your dog if you have one, or plant a garden, or cook. I think you get my point. There's seeing, and then there's *seeing what you're seeing with total awareness.* Depending on your level of seeing, it makes a big difference in not only what you see, but in how what you're seeing affects you and makes you feel.

Remember, our brain chemicals are being stimulated by not only external things and events, but by how we perceive them. And if we want to get those neurons fired up in such a way that we get the "rewards" those transmitters can give us, we need to be fully present to make that happen. The more present we are, the more we can work with our brain to help it maintain mental wellness and acuity. We and our brain need to be working in tandem. The more we value this organ that governs our entire nervous system, and is said to have as many neurons as there are stars in the Milky Way, the more our brain can show us what it's got to offer—and it's got a whole lot more than we're tapping into. Mindfulness is the gateway to a healthier brain for sure, and a more expansive one. As mysterious as the brain is, Mindfulness, I believe, can help us know more about it and the brilliance of which it is capable.

What we know about the brain is that it can change throughout our life. By practicing Mindfulness, and consciously regulating our thoughts and emotions in present time, which supports emotional intelligence, we can grow more neurons and create new pathways in our brain. In our practicing of Mindfulness, we can begin to actually be the arbiters of not only changing our brain, but also the chemicals in it. And who knows what else we can come to know and learn about this three-pound enigmatic mass and what it will be capable of doing in the future as we continue to evolve.

So, do you want to be more present? Do you want to experience more heightened states of awareness? Do you want your senses to be more stimulated? Do you want to feel fully alive in every fiber of your being, and experience those "feel-good" chemicals that can make you feel a type of euphoria that is thought to only be possible with certain drugs? As Thich Nhat Hahn said in the quote above, "You can establish yourself in the present to touch the wonders of life that are available in the moment," but you must be present to experience those wonders.

Being alive is a miracle, but you must be fully present to know this, and when you are, you are attuned to the mystical, the spiritual mystery of life.

Sit quietly

Close your eyes

Put your hand on your heart

Feel your breath

Say silently "I am present

I am grateful to be alive"

MINDFULNESS & MYSTICISM

CHAPTER 2

DEMYSTIFYING MYSTICISM

What does mysticism really mean?
It means the way to attain knowledge.
It's close to philosophy except in philosophy you go horizontally
while in mysticism you go vertically.

— ELIE WIESEL

A totally un-mystical world would be
a world totally blind and insane.

— ALDOUS HUXLEY

One of the definitions of "mysticism" is "union or direct communion with ultimate reality reported by mystics." In the book, Mysticism, Evelyn Underhill's seminal work on this subject, she says that "mysticism in its pure form, is the science of ultimates, the science of union with the Absolute, and nothing else, and the mystic is the person who attains to this union, not the person who talks about it. Not to know about but to Be is the mark of the real initiate."

Underhill wrote many books on mysticism and was the first women to address the clergy of the Church of England. Here, she describes a mystical experience she had:

"The first thing I found out was exalted and indescribable beauty in the most squalid places. I still remember walking down the Notting Hill main road and observing the landscape (which was completely sordid) with joy and astonishment. Even the movement of traffic had something universal and sublime about it. Of course, that does not last – but the after-flavor of it does, and now and then one catches it again. When one does catch it, it is so real that to look upon it as wrong would be an unthinkable absurdity. At the same time, one sees the world at those moments as "energized by the invisible" that there is no temptation to rest in mere enjoyment of the visible." (The Letters of Evelyn Underhill).

Underhill's mystical experience, which she describes as "exalted" and "sublime," is something similar to what many people have felt, including myself, but perhaps kept it to themselves, or didn't know how to articulate it. When I went to a therapist to talk about my euphoric episodes, I didn't know what to make of them at the time.

I've explained the chemicals in our brain that can produce euphoria, and the type of bliss people can feel on drugs or alcohol, but I'm interested in exploring further an area where I strongly feel we can understand ourselves better. These unusual or inexplicable feelings and sensations that might be hard to put into words, and that's mysticism, which has been mostly thought of as esoteric, or only understood by mystics.

Mysticism has also been defined as "the practice of religious ecstasies" and a "religious experience during alternate states of consciousness." Does that then mean it can only be experienced through religion? Evelyn Underhill was "walking down the Notting Hill main road" when she had a mystical experience, and someone like primatologist, Jane Goodall, described having a mystical experience in a forest in the following passage:

"Lost in awe at the beauty around me, I must have slipped into a state of heightened awareness. It is hard, impossible really to put into words the moment of truth that suddenly came upon me then. Even the mystics are unable to describe their brief flashes of spiritual ecstasy. It seemed to me, as I struggled afterward to recall the experience, the self was utterly absent: I and the chimpanzees, the earth and trees and air, seemed to merge, to become one with the spirit power of life itself. The air was filled with a feathered symphony, the evensong of birds. I heard new frequencies in their music and also in singing insects' voices, notes so high and sweet I was amazed. Never had I been so intensely aware of the shape, the color of the individual leaves, the varied patterns of the veins that made each one unique. Scents were clear as well, easily identifiable: fermenting, overripe fruit; waterlogged earth; cold, wet bark; the damp odor of chimpanzee hair, and yes, my own too. And the aromatic scent of young, crushed leaves was almost overpowering." (Jane Goodall's Reason for Hope: A Spiritual Journey.)

Neither Goodall or Underhill's mystical experiences are described as "religious," even though a mystical experience can be called religious when one experiences an alternate state of consciousness, or spiritual awareness during a religious activity like praying, or "davening," which is Jewish prayer recitations and meditations many Hasidic Jews practice. I remember one time when I stood next to a beautiful orthodox woman at the Western Wall, also called the Wailing Wall in Jerusalem, which is a sacred place of prayer and pilgrimage to the Jewish

people, and I was captivated by how she was swaying her
body backward and forward over and over again as she
silently mouthed the words from a small prayer book she
held close to her face. Her cheeks were bright pink, and
she seemed as though she were in a trance. I found myself
wondering whether she was more connected to God than
I was because she seemed so devoted to her religion, and
the religious practices of it. I answered my own question,
and it was "no." I felt that what is spiritual or holy for
me lies deep within my heart and soul, and my connection to God, or what I view as Divine, does not require
me to devote myself to a particular religion, or pray like
anyone else does. How I express my spirituality, or connect to what I perceive as holy and sacred, is personal,
and I needn't compare myself to others in how I choose
to express it, which is why mysticism resonates for me so
deeply.

Although mysticism has been defined as "the practice of religious ecstasies" or a "religious experience," it
is an "extraordinary experience and state of mind," as
Underhill described it, and we can have it, whether we're
engaged in a religious activity like prayer, walking down
a "squalid road", or in a forest with chimpanzees. I believe we can have a mystical experience taking out the
garbage, or brushing our teeth. There is no place where
we cannot have an extraordinary experience in our mind,
which Goodall describes as "flashes of spiritual ecstasy"

because it can happen without us planning for it. That flash can occur at the most unlikely place or time, and not only while sitting in a church or temple, where we might assume is the most likely place to experience "religious ecstasies." Maybe we believe that if we give ourselves over to God, or a Divine entity especially if we are in an act of prayer or a place of worship we are more open to receive spiritual ecstasy, which we might be. But, how about waking up in the morning open to receive it, instead of waiting for it to happen, or assume it can only happen in certain places, doing certain things?

We cannot be open to receiving anything related to a mystical experience if we don't believe in it, and most people don't. If you have never had even the slightest "altered state of consciousness," then maybe you don't believe that euphoria or ecstasy is something you can experience other than through religion, relying on substances, using your devices, while having an orgasm during sex, or maybe from an adrenaline rush, which a mountain climber can experience.

Psychologist Abraham Maslow describes a "peak experience" as moments of "highest happiness and fulfillment." Why is it that we feel we have to rely on something, or do something unusual to have these peak experiences instead of believing that all we have to do is be present, aware, and available for them to happen? As Goodall says about her mystical experience, "she must have slipped into a state of heightened awareness."

If Buddha became enlightened while sitting under a tree, what makes us think we have to do something out of the ordinary for that to happen? Yes, he set himself on a path to understand human suffering, but he went deep within himself for the answers, and that's where he realized enlightenment. We are far too busy looking for answers outside of ourselves, and relying too much on distractions, stimulants, materialism, and every possible thing we can think of that we believe will give us the high, the rush, the peak experience, or that feeling of ecstasy we're longing for.

Drug addicts want the high. They want to numb their pain, and once they experience the numbing from their pain, and the high in place of it, they want more. Whether it's physical pain or emotional, not dealing with the cause of the pain or the suffering it perpetuates keeps it alive and ongoing, and that's why so many people reach out for drugs as the easy way to numb it, or "kill" it off, which means possibly killing themselves in the process.

If an addict could mainline straight into a direct source of ecstasy, other than a drug, and have it fill their veins with bliss, they probably would be willing to sell their soul for it. Who doesn't want to feel bliss? We all do, but if it's for reasons other than to experience "heightened awareness" like Jane Goodall did, or "exalted and indescribable beauty" like Evelyn Underhill felt walking down a "squalid" street," then we will continue to desperately desire bliss to fill a deep, gaping hole in our souls.

Each of us, in our own way, is in search of something greater, or just "something" that can give greater meaning to our lives. We are longing to become whole, to unite with that something that will connect us to what we are desperately longing for, and what could it be that our soul deeply yearns for? Perhaps it's that we are "In Search of the Miraculous," the title of a book by Russian philosopher and esotericist, P. D. Ouspensky, which was based on his meetings with spiritual teacher and mystic, George Gurdjieff, who taught him an ancient, esoteric system of self-development known as the "Fourth Way." This "Fourth Way," in essence, was a teaching of working on oneself, or as Ouspensky called it, "self-remembering." It is geared for "inner development" and emphasizes that people "live in a state referred to as semi-hypnotic, waking sleep, while higher levels of consciousness, virtue, unity of will are possible." What the Fourth Way aims for is to "transform man into what he ought to be."

And what is it that we "ought to be?" Human beings are always yearning for more, and tirelessly in search of something that causes us a never-ending hunger we cannot properly feed, or satiate? Maybe we can better feed and satisfy our hunger if we know exactly what it is we are hungry for. Could it be that this insatiable hunger is from wanting a deeper understanding of why we were

born, and what we were born to do? We desperately want
to know the true meaning and purpose of our existence,
but we can't unless we strip ourselves bare of all the things
that have deceived us from the purest essence of our soul,
and drugs and alcohol, or any type of escapism can inten-
sify that deception. Does our soul not desire to (re)unite
with the divine because it knows that it entered our body
born from that which is "invisible," and when we have a
mystical experience, we are, in fact, being energized by
what we cannot see but know deep in our hearts is most
real and true? This is what Underhill means when she
says, "one sees the world at those moments as energized
by the invisible, that there is no temptation to rest in mere
enjoyment of the visible."

We live more comfortably with the "visible," or what
we can see and know with certainty. Mysticism can't offer
us that. If you're someone who needs empirical proof, or
science-based facts on why something "is" or how it "came
to be," then believing in that which is invisible probably
won't be enough for you to go by, or trust. And, that's
exactly why mysticism gets a bad wrap: because it can't be
scientifically proven, although some people might feel differently. Their mystical experiences can feel as real as anything that science can prove to be true, but if mysticism
gets reduced to an explanation that "it is only one's brain"
that is creating the experience, and so it is not considered
real, which is why it can be called "delusional," isn't it then

provable by machines that can measure neural patterns of someone having a mystical experience? We know something happens in our brain when we are having a mystical experience, or in a heightened state of consciousness, but what, exactly, can we can say it is? Calling it "mysticism" or a "mystical experience" might not give it the credibility people need to take it seriously.

It may not be easy to clarify what mysticism means, be it scientifically, or by its definition, which there are many. One of them is that mysticism is "union with God," or as Underhill says, "union with reality." Our relationship to God, or reality, is completely subjective and personal, and can be described by how we perceive either one. We can say that we believe in God, but if one were to say they saw God, and it was a mystical experience for them, not a religious one, that would be more readily questioned or doubted. "How can you see God?" they might be asked? After all, He is invisible (or She if you believe God is a woman). The universal, archetypal image that most people ascribe to God is that of an old man in a long robe with white hair, and a beard.

Do we assume this is what God looks like because He has been depicted this way in paintings and biblical texts? We can talk to God through prayer, and that's considered normal and acceptable, but if we say we actually see God, or that He/She came to us in a vision, and it wasn't an old man with white hair and beard, you might run the risk of being called mad or delusional. This quote by Alan Watts, takes it even further:

"Jesus Christ knew he was God. So, wake up and find out eventually who you really are. In our culture, of course, they'll say you're crazy and you're blasphemous, and they'll either put you in jail or in a nut house (which is pretty much the same thing). However, if you wake up in India and tell your friends and relations, 'My goodness, I've just discovered that I'm God,' they'll laugh and say, 'Oh, congratulations, at last you found out.'"

Mysticism is real, and anything but delusional. Whatever experiences we have that connect us to God, the Divine, the absolute, source, oneness, or whatever you choose to call it, is ours to have, and nobody has a right to tell us they aren't real. The mystical experience is not something that can only be experienced by mystics. They may be people who seek to know "spiritual truths that are beyond the intellect," as mystics are described, but the mystical experience is available for anyone to have, if they are open to it.

And how do we stay open to it? We walk down a street like Evelyn Underhill did, and observe what we see with "joy and astonishment," or we lose ourselves in the beauty all around us, as Jane Goodall describes before she "must have slipped into a state of heightened awareness."

Mysticism will remain a mystery to those who choose not to see themselves in union with God, reality, chimpanzees, the earth, trees, air, and everything around us. And, if you are not present, you cannot feel the "oneness" of all that exists. We are "one." There is no separation, other than how we perceive ourselves and this life. Whether it's what we can see, or the invisible, we must trust that there is something greater we are meant to know, and as Evelyn Underhill says, "When one does catch it, it is so real that to look upon it as wrong would be an unthinkable absurdity."

Walk this earth

Eyes wide open

See all that you can

Closely and carefully

Then look further

MINDFULNESS & MYSTICISM

CHAPTER 3

AWAKEN NOW

And once you are awake,
you shall remain awake eternally.

— FRIEDRICH NIETZSCHE

What does it mean to be awake? To rouse ourselves from sleep and go out in our day, doing what we do? For many, that is being sufficiently awake. They view their life as something to do, and expect to be fulfilled for their doing.

We have an expectation of life, a very big one. We want it to satisfy us and make us happy, which is a reasonable expectation to have. After all, why shouldn't life bring us joy, and provide us with what we want? We are good people (those who live with kindness and compassion); and we work (those who work); and believe in God, or a Divine being (those who believe in God, or a Divine being); and we pray (those who pray); and we give to others (those who give to others); and we care about the world (those who care about the world); and we come from a place of love in all that we do (those who come from a place of love in all that they do).

All of this constitutes being alive, but it doesn't necessarily mean that you are awake. Being awake means how aware you are in all that you do. You may be alive, but that does not mean you are awake, consciously.

Being awake consciously means that you are fully present. And being fully present means you are consciously aware of how present you are. As I said in Chapter 1 - Behold Mindfulness. We can be awake doing, but if we are not fully aware of who we are in our doing, and how conscious we are doing whatever we are engaged in, then we're just not awake enough. That's right. You're either awake fully, or you're not. And, if you're not, you might not even be aware of it. Don't feel bad or berate yourself if you feel you fall into the "less awake" category because most people don't know they are not fully awake. That doesn't mean you can't awaken more. You can, if you want to. Wanting to awaken more means you have an awareness of the possibility that there is always more to awaken to, and there is always more to be aware of. When you make a conscious choice to awaken more, veils begin to lift before you, and the art of seeing begins to change.

As Thoreau said, "The question is not what you look at that matters, it's what you see." And to add to that, poet Jonathan Swift puts it this way: "Vision is the art of seeing what is invisible to others."

Seeing, is indeed, an art form. How we see what we are looking at can ignite our imagination in such a way that it not only fires up our neurons, but it can stimulate a deeper understanding of what we are beholding. Whether it's an image captured by a photographer, an artist's portrait of a person, or a still life of a bowl of grapes, how something is seen can influence what is captured so uniquely, it cannot only evoke a myriad of feelings and emotions in someone who looks at it, but it can also awaken something deep within them that had laid dormant or asleep. I have found myself looking at art and being moved to tears. Botticelli's Birth of Venus captures divine love in a way that feels transcendent. When I look at it, I can see myself in Venus. She mirrors to me my own maturity as a woman, stripped bare of any falsehood. She stands naked in a seashell as authentic as you can be.

And then there's one of the most viewed masterpieces in the world, Leonardo Da Vinci's Mona Lisa. I remember feeling such anticipation when I saw it at the Louvre Museum in Paris. I could barely make my way through the crowd, but when I was finally able to see her image behind glass, I felt like I could spend hours getting lost in her face. I wanted to look deep into it and interpret her elusive smile in a way that made sense to me, and it did, in a mysterious kind of way. Perhaps it was Da Vinci's ability to capture what was visible only to him, and "invisible to others" that beckons us to look more deeply to see what the artist saw, and if we do, we share the mystical experience with them in our own way.

This is what Mindfulness does for us. It holds us in present moment awareness, as if whispering in our ear, "Stay here in this moment, and look more deeply into what you are seeing. You will see much more than just what is on the surface."

We can become very present when something captures our attention, like the Mona Lisa. But not everyone is patient or interested to look beyond her elusive smile, and get lost in the moment as if it never ends. And that's another magical thing Mindfulness does. It makes a moment feel as if it's standing still, and time, as we know it, has no beginning or end, but just now and now can feel eternal.

Once we step out of the moment, and allow ourselves to be swept up in an energy that feels less transcendent or mystical, we return to life more rooted in the practical, which is how we live most of the time. That's understandable, considering we need to get things done, and live our lives adhering to time, schedules, and commitments. But, where we let the mystical slip out of our grasp is we forget that even in the practical, day-to-day doing, we must make room for the possibility of heightened awareness, which doesn't mean we're doing things floating ten feet off the ground and less focused on what needs to be accomplished well and efficiently.

No, on the contrary, being fully awake, and having a more heightened awareness, means that we can participate in life not only as grounded, sensible human beings, but we can also be deeply aware of everything and everyone around us simultaneously. This means that everything we do is done with a conscious awareness of how we are doing it; therefore, it makes us more thoughtful, kind, compassionate, sensitive, creative, and highly aware and attuned people. But we must train ourselves to be more present because life will always pull us out of present moment awareness, and most of the time we are completely unaware that it is happening. Mindfulness helps keep us awake, and if we are about to slip out of the moment and become less conscious, it gently nudges us to stay present and aware, or, if needed, can give us a strong push, even a shove if we're really falling asleep at the wheel and about to do something foolish, or even catastrophic. This may sound like we never get respite from being awake, but we have sleep for that. We are not meant to be in a state of slumber during our awake time, and if one feels tired, and in need of mental rest, that's what naps are for.

In order to achieve a more heightened state of awareness, we must be awake enough to know that our awareness can be heightened more than it is. What if your awareness could be heightened to such a degree that you felt as if you had some type of extra-sensory perception, and what you were seeing and feeling went beyond the senses? This is how a mystical experience can be described going beyond what we sense from the everyday physical world. The "oneness" that people have felt when they were in a heightened state of awareness can feel like you are experiencing something that goes beyond the five senses and can seem ineffable. Could it be that the more awake we are, the more of our senses we can access, and perhaps there are more than just five?

If our senses help us understand the world around us, it's possible to think that there is more for us to know, and the physical world is the dimension that allows us to see, but we must go beyond just what we're looking at, and again, as Thoreau said, "The question is not what you look at that matters, it's what you see." It could be that the more awake we are, the more we see, and the more we see, the more awake we become, and that is when we can access other senses we may not have known we had until we are able to experience them. According to Barry C. Smith, professor of philosophy at the University of London's School of Advanced Study, we have "somewhere between 22 and 33 senses" and it's the way our five traditional senses interact that creates more. Could it be that in order for Evelyn Underhill or Jane Goodall to have experienced their mystical experiences, they had to be so present and aware, they allowed their senses to interact in such a way that something truly awe-inspiring happened?

Seeing the beauty and wonder all around us, can, indeed, inspire awe, but only if we're awake enough for that to happen. You are not going to see the beauty and wonder all around you if you're not awake enough to even appreciate it. There is so much beauty around us all the time that if we were to stop and be fully present in the moments of our life, we might be in a constant state of ecstasy but maybe that's just too much for us to handle. After all, how could we possibly sustain a state of bliss all the time, and not be completely high out of our mind? Is there such a thing? To be too high, naturally? I mean, we do seek the high, or those peak experiences Maslow spoke about, and we look for that feeling of euphoria or bliss outside of ourselves all the time. We like being high, whether it's through drugs, alcohol, or the adrenaline rush we go after by exercising, and doing things like extreme adventures that are risky, or even dangerous.

But, if we're awake, fully, and I mean to the point that we don't just look, but really see what we're looking at with our five senses functioning at their optimum, and interacting with each other in ways that feel as if there is no separation from the oneness that is all, then maybe we can experience higher states of consciousness on a more regular basis, and that can feel normal to us. That means we are open to the mystical and show up in all of the moments of our life ready to receive something extraordinary and awe-inspiring. We live our life so separate from the extraordinary most of the time, we just accept it as the way life is supposed to be lived. To quote the title of my first book, Says Who? who said that life is meant to be lived in any other way than awe-inspiring?

If we choose to awaken more, then we can know what lies beyond the slumber of our unconsciousness. How can we experience "heightened awareness" if we are not awake enough to even know that these states of consciousness are possible? They are for those who choose to awaken beyond the limits of their mind. Be aware of your level of awareness, and strive to awaken more. As Ouspensky said so succinctly, "When one realizes one is asleep, at that moment one is already half-awake."

I am awake
But I must awaken more
To know that I've been asleep
Far too long

MINDFULNESS & MYSTICISM

CHAPTER 4

TRANSCENDING THE ORDINARY

Everyone wants to lead an extraordinary life.

— AUGUSTUS

My powers are ordinary.
Only my application brings me success.

— ISAAC NEWTON

One of the biggest fears many people have is that they are ordinary, or that they live ordinary lives. We admire people who do extraordinary things but neglect to consider what Isaac Newton says in the quote above, that their "powers are ordinary" and it is the "application" of ordinary powers that brings success.

How can we attempt to experience anything extraordinary if we perceive ourselves as ordinary? Let's start with this: We already are extraordinary, but we diminish our extraordinariness by constantly telling ourselves we have no special or distinctive features or characteristics. It's fine to consider yourself normal, or average, or just your typical person doing every day, common things. But, even in your normal, average, typical, or everyday ways that you do what you do, there is something unique and remarkable about you that you may not even be aware of because you consider yourself anything but special or unusual.

There are some theories around parenting that say we shouldn't over-praise our children, or even praise them at all. Saying things like "good job!" or "way to go!" is believed to be over said whenever a child does something good, or worthy of acknowledgment, and some psychologists believe it can do more harm than good. If acknowledging your child for every single thing they do right or good is met with an immediate "good job!" or "way to go!" then, yes, I imagine they would expect it, and perhaps feel unacknowledged if it wasn't said when they did anything that wasn't a mistake or a misstep in some way.

For many parents, they believe that praising their child is the best way to build good self-esteem, and what child, or even adult, doesn't want to hear that they've done something good or well? Who doesn't want to hear a nice compliment? I would think we all do, but that doesn't mean we don't resist believing it and tell ourselves silently that we don't deserve praise or adulation, even when we do.

That is because there is something within us that does feel ordinary, or we wouldn't have a constant inner critic, which we do to varying degrees. That inner critic can be much harsher than telling us that we're average or common, which for some people would be considered gentle. The way we measure our self-worth is by our successes and failures, and even if you praised your children early on, life will do a pretty sufficient job of letting them know how well they do, or don't do, no matter how much praise, or over-praising, you gave them.

Yes, life will do all that it can to remind us of our ordinariness by showing us how powerful and daunting it is. And, if we try and prove that we too are powerful, well, we know that life can slam us down again and again, reminding us that we are not only ordinary, but also not as powerful as we'd like to believe. That is why we are left feeling ordinary and powerless by what life has shown us, or feel life has done to us. For many, they are defeated by what can be perceived as life's insurmountable power and resort to living not just as an ordinary human being, but more like a beaten down one.

Living an ordinary life can feel perfectly acceptable, and if your life feels ordinary for you, and you're comfortable with that, then perhaps there is no need to aspire for more. But why not go for something more? Why not desire a life that is more than the one you have, and I don't just mean having material possessions? We can dream about living a life that seems beyond what is meant for us, or even realistic. And we can fantasize what it would be like having what other people have, but deep inside we feel we don't deserve it. Where does this lack of deserving come from? Even if you were one of those children who were told you can do no wrong, and praised endlessly by your parents, you can still feel that you are ordinary or average and don't deserve anything more than what a typically average person should get.

This type of distorted thinking occupies the minds of millions of people, and they accept these types of limited beliefs about themselves. Their lives might seem ordinary, but what is most average about them are their thoughts, and that can change at any time. If you think you're ordinary, and deserve what seems befitting of an ordinary person, then that is what you will manifest for yourself.

As we know, there are many people who came from very ordinary, or humble beginnings, and yet, they manifested a life for themselves that was anything but ordinary. Joan of Arc grew up a peasant in medieval France and started hearing the voices of saints from a young age. When she was 18, she believed that she was chosen by God to lead France to victory in its ongoing war with England. And in our modern day, JK Rowling, author of the hugely popular Harry Potter series was born in a lowly English family. She not only battled depression, but also had suicidal tendencies. It's been said that she was a highly imaginative child, and for all we know she could have experienced the mystical as she delved into such inventive and visionary realms to dream up the world of Harry Potter. Both of these women are great examples of people who possessed "ordinary powers" as Newton said, and applied them to achieve success in what they set out to do.

When we don't accept ordinary, or allow ourselves to be complacent living an ordinary life, we will find ourselves moving towards something that feels more special, even wondrous. I remember being an avid daydreamer as a child. I don't recall perceiving myself, or my life, as ordinary, although there wasn't anything exceptional about how I grew up. But it was my mind that imagined places that felt more magical, even mystical to me, and I loved going there. If I, for one minute, thought that I couldn't allow my mind to experience those imaginative places because I didn't actually live there, or there wasn't anything in my reality that mimicked some of the daydreams or fantasies I had, I don't believe I could have written the contemplative poems I began writing as a young girl, or danced for hours in my living room, pretending I was performing at the Ballets Russes in Paris.

When we are present and aware, and feel ourselves fully alive, we transcend the ordinary by letting our mind carry us to places that are far beyond the limitations of everyday, boring, or monotonous thinking. And, if we get in the habit of opening ourselves up to the beauty and awe that is around us, then that is what we see, even if on the surface life may seem simple or ordinary. What we see is through our own perceptions, and our perceptions are shaped and altered by not just what we look at, but, as Thoreau said, by what we see. And when we do this, we are open to the mystical, and ready to receive something extraordinary and awe-inspiring. Maybe that is why Joan of Arc heard what she believed were the "voices of saints" that told her to act valiantly, which she did. As I said in Chapter 3 – Awaken Now, "We live our life so separate from the extraordinary most of the time, we just accept it as the way life is supposed to be lived." No, life is meant to be lived as wondrous and remarkable as you want it to be, and if you believe that ordinary is how you are meant to live because it's all you've ever experienced, then know that if at any time you "apply" your powers, because you have them, you can transcend the limitations of routine, day-to-day thinking, and something very mystical might be in store for you. But above all, as Goethe said, "Trust yourself, then you will know how to live."

Am I ordinary
Or am I extraordinary
I am both
But I choose extraordinary
To lift my ordinariness
To extraordinary heights

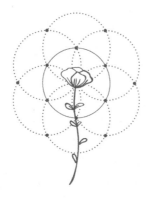

MINDFULNESS & MYSTICISM

CHAPTER 5

DIVINE THOUGHT
ILLUMINATION

I am a moment illuminating eternity...
I am affirmation...I am ecstasy.

— ALEXANDER SCRIABIN

Listen my love, illumination is eternal.
Now is always evolving. As there are billions of stars, there
are billions of steps. As there are billions of souls, there are
billions of ways to grow.

— RUMI

Divine illumination is a doctrine associated with theologian, and Christian philosopher, Saint Augustine, who spoke of the important role of divine illumination in our thoughts. He said: "The mind needs to be enlightened by light from outside itself, so that it can participate in truth, because it is not itself the nature of truth." Augustine also said: "You will light my lamp, Lord. You hear nothing true from me which you have not first told me" (Augustine Confessions).

Divine illumination played an important role in Greek philosophy, and near the end of the thirteenth century, Christian medieval philosophers debunked Augustine's theory that the only way one can experience divine illumination is through "supernatural assistance." According to the Stanford Encyclopedia of Philosophy, it goes on to explain that divine illumination is a theory on which "the mind must regularly rely on this assistance, in order to complete its ordinary cognitive activity: otherwise, an occasional mystical experience might suffice to confirm a theory of divine illumination."

Even from a modern-day perspective, divine illumination, like mysticism, is still referred to in a more esoteric or religious context, and both considered something that is experienced through supernatural assistance. The whole notion of "supernatural assistance" conjures up the need to be helped in order to experience divine illumination, which I view as thinking that is guided by light. Is this an arbitrary decision for us to guide our own thoughts, or must we be assisted in order to think thoughts that are "godly" or "heavenly?"

I have thoughts that I consider heavenly and beatific, and if you ask me where do those thoughts come from, I can quickly answer, "From my own mind." Do I rule out the possibility that I am having "supernatural assistance?" No, I don't, but I'd like to think I play a greater role in deciding what type of "illumined" thoughts I want to occupy my mind, and take responsibility for choosing to believe thoughts that either enhance my light, or diminish it.

Sometimes those heavenly type of thoughts come unexpectedly, and other times I consciously choose to think them. When I have them, they can make me feel a type of bliss and euphoria I've been speaking about, and that euphoria is what got me to go to a therapist to ask why I was experiencing it. At the time, it did seem odd and strange, and I, myself, did not know why I was occasionally experiencing a type of feeling that could only be described by comparing it to a highly addictive analgesic drug, and one I had never even tried. I was young and had no reference point for what I was experiencing, but I wanted answers, which, unfortunately, I did not get. So, I pretty much went on my merry way, accepting that there really wasn't an answer for my euphoric episodes, but today I feel quite differently.

I was an open vessel to experience that euphoria. Although I didn't ask for divine illumination, or a mystical experience, I definitely received it, and I believe that each of us can experience divine illumination, mystical experiences, and higher states of consciousness if we want to. Just being open to the possibility of it already means that if, or when, it happens, you won't be frightened or confused by it, and if you believe that you were "assisted supernaturally" by something outside of yourself, so be it.

Can we be influenced by external illumination, be it "God lighting our lamp," as Augustine felt we needed? Yes, our mind can be "enlightened by light from outside of itself," but it can also be enlightened from a light that exists within. I'm aware that there will always be differing opinions, or many philosophical and religious theories about what exists in our soul, and what exists outside of it. I am bringing Mindfulness and mysticism into this conversation so that we may take a closer look at how they play a significant role in keeping our minds illumined, and by doing so, we can "participate in truth" as Augustine said, by being awake and aware enough to even know what that truth is.

In order for our minds to be "lit up," we must be in an active state of awareness, as I spoke about in Chapter 3 - Awaken Now. But, if we're not aware of our tendencies to sleep-walk through life, what chance do we have to experience any type of illumination or higher states of consciousness?

I suppose we can assume that if God wants to "light

our lamp," as Augustine spoke of, He will. But, if we aren't even aware that our light is dim, or completely turned off, then what difference does it make? Illumination, whether we turn it on ourselves, or ask for God's help, is something we need to be aware of, and know that it is a most necessary beacon to light the way on this complex life journey. We need our thoughts to be illumined so that our mind can possess a clarity that feels as if we are guided by nothing other than the divine, and only then can truth be known to us, and by this, I mean the sacred truths of life, which the mystical journey helps you to discover.

I'm not concerned with how you find or access your light. Is it really any of our business which religious, or non-religious well anyone drinks from to quench their soul's thirst for a greater, or more sacred meaning of this life? It's not having a yearning for meaning that worries me, but the belief that drugs, alcohol, or something outside of ourselves is all we need to connect us to something higher, and that's enough. Maybe there is no meaning needed to explain this life, and drugs, alcohol, or whatever we use to lighten our mental load is how we can live our days less burdened and tortured by the possibility that there isn't anything more for us to know or understand. Perhaps. But for me, I seek to know more, and feel that if we choose to be awake, present, and aware in our life, we not only stand a chance of having "awe inspiring" moments, but also mystical experiences. There are profound truths for us to know, and these truths of the universe are revealed to those ready to know it.

Yes, this life is a great mystery, and is it possible for us to know what this earth plane, the universe, and the entire cosmos are really all about? Who's to say that before we take our last breath here, we don't have a major epiphany, an aha moment, a brain chemical blast of euphoria so mind-blowing that everything in a split second makes total sense to us, and our soul parts from the body it has used, and we return to the divine light, the illumination from whence we came.

I do hold that possibility in my mind's eye, but what I want to encourage is for us not to wait for that to happen but instead use divine thought illumination in our day-to-day lives. Please know that I'm not saying we have to have our minds blown constantly unless you would like that, and I have no doubt you can experience as many mind-blowing moments as you wish. Be my guest to have your mind blown as much as you want to, but how do you think that's going to happen? And don't you want to comprehend what your mind is taking in, and be able to explain or articulate it as best you can? I think a mystical experience can be completely mind-blowing, but what's so beautiful about it is how some people who experienced them were able to articulate it in such clear, picturesque ways. Both Evelyn Underhill and Jane Goodall explained their mystical experiences in a way that didn't seem unrealistic, or at all "delusional." It was something extraordinary that happened to them because they were simply present and aware in their lives, just as we can be.

What I gleaned from both of their mystical experiences was that they were very present in what they were doing. Their minds were nowhere other than where they were; Underhill walking down a street and Goodall in a forest. It wasn't that they were asking for a mystical experience; it was that they were present, aware, and open enough for it to happen. And, that's how I believe we can experience "union with a reality" that is transcendent by being fully present and open for it to happen. By being more present, we are more open, and by being more present and open, we are elevating our awareness, which raises our consciousness. So why wouldn't we aspire to raise both our awareness and consciousness, which can only increase the possibility of receiving the mystical?

Levels and states of consciousness vary, and can be altered by many things, depending on what we're doing, and again, how awake and aware we are in our doing. I feel that even by making a conscious decision to be more conscious, we can better prepare ourselves to experience higher states of consciousness and have a mystical experience by choice, which I will go into further later. That means if I am gazing at something I find beautiful or pleasing, like a sunrise or sunset, a flower opening, or the undulating motion of waves in an ocean, it stimulates the neurotransmitters in my brain, which then releases those "feel-good" chemicals I've spoken about. By being fully present with what I am not just looking at, but actually seeing, I then can go deeper into the experience. This is when everything becomes divine, and a feeling of oneness can be realized.

But it's important, as I said, to be present in the moments of our life. By being fully aware, we can not only keep our thoughts illumined, but we are also cognizant of when a thought appears that is inclined to disrupt a conscious state of illumination, which happens when we shift into fear or doubt. When this occurs, we can choose to remain in divine illumination, as difficult as it may seem. You see, we have a choice to always stay in the light of our existence, and that means holding thoughts in our mind that support that light. But, as Chardin said, we are "spiritual beings having a human experience," and it will remain challenging for us to stay aligned with the spiritual wisdom that is deep within us, which is why practicing Mindfulness is so extremely helpful and important. We will be reminded again and again that we are susceptible to forgetting our true nature by how readily we accept thoughts that tell us we are less than who we truly are. I don't necessarily agree with Augustine when he says that the mind "is not itself the nature of truth," which is why it needs God's help.

When we are fully present and aware in a moment,

we are more in "the nature of truth" than not, meaning we are accepting "what is," instead of resisting it, and that, in itself, is more aligned with our "true nature," which in a Taoist sense ("living simply, honestly, and in harmony with nature") allows us to flow with all that is true in the universe. If we don't resist what is most true, and stay connected to our nature, we would be in harmony with all of nature, and isn't that the nature of truth, to trust our own intuitive intelligence, which is "innate in the human mind?"

The best way to gauge when we are slipping away from our true nature, which, I believe, wants nothing more than to be aligned with all that exists, the oneness we can experience when we feel unified and not separate from anything or anyone is when our thoughts become less illumined. Mindfulness helps us know when a thought is pulling us way from the truth, as Rumi says in the quote above that, "Illumination is eternal."

Pick a thought that pleases you
Imagine that thought
Radiating with white light
Growing wider and wider
Reverberating farther and farther out
Imagine that you are
The creator of this thought
And each thought that follows
Tell yourself that you can
Create illumined thoughts
Whenever you wish to

MINDFULNESS & MYSTICISM

CHAPTER 6

LIVING A DIVINE LIFE

The Divine Light is always in man, presenting itself to the senses and to the comprehension, but man rejects it.

— GIORDANO BRUNO

This life is not man's own show; if he becomes personally and emotionally involved in the very complicated cosmic drama, he reaps inevitable suffering for having distorted the divine 'plot.'

— PARAMAHANSA YOGANANDA

Before I talk about what it means to live a Divine Life, I'd like to ask you, would you like to live one? I am taking you now from the ordinary to the divine because I believe you can make that leap, and what I'm asking you really is do you want to live your life different from how you are living it right now, maybe more glorious, more sublime, even more blissful? Perhaps you consider your life already divine, and for you that might mean your life is pretty delightful, and everything is going well. If that's the case, wonderful!

But would you like to experience even more delight, and maybe take that delight into areas that might give your life greater meaning? As I said previously, not everyone desires greater meaning in their life. If you're religious, maybe your particular religion gives your life the exact meaning you require, and there is no need for more. And for those who aren't religious, they might derive meaning in their life from things that are considered "spiritual, not religious," which is a phrase we hear more often, and means you don't choose religion to define your spiritual growth, so therefore aren't affiliated with one.

Personally, I think we should leave one another alone to quench our soul's thirst for a greater, or more sacred meaning of this life however we choose to, as I said in Chapter 5 - Divine Thought Illumination. Historically, we have been known to do horrible things to our fellow man over how we choose to light up our soul, and the beliefs or paths we follow to do it. If Christ, Muhammad,

Krishna, Buddha, Joseph Smith, Confucius, or any saintly being reaches deep into your soul, and makes you feel that they lead the way to God for you, or are the embodiment of God, I embrace you, and hope that you can embrace me if I have chosen a different path than you to access God or whatever represents the divine to me. And, if I tell you what the divine looks like, which might be different from what it looks like to you, please don't be judgmental, cruel, or hateful. Easier said than done, right?

We do judge one another for our different beliefs, especially around religion, so let us put our beliefs aside and focus on something that each of us can experience, regardless of who or what we believe in, and that's living a life that is inspired by what all religions tell us. If we take the common themes of each of the major religions: Judaism, Christianity, Islam, Hinduism, Buddhism, Sikhism, Confucianism, Shinto, and Taoism (if I left your religion out, please know that all religions are welcome here) and focus on what they teach us, this is pretty much what we get:

1. Believe in love.
2. Honor God.
3. Don't do evil, selfish, and destructive things.
4. Do good, loving, and kind things for your neighbor.

That sounds simple enough to do. Where it veers onto a slippery slope is when the definition of God comes into play, and for some religions there are many gods, not just one, which is called Polytheism. For some people, they believe you should be accepting only of people of your own religion who believe in the same God, and even if those religions practice monotheism, a belief in one God, which Judaism, Christianity, and Islam share in this common tradition, some religions can be very competitive, intolerant, and even merciless, and that's where the difficulty lies. Even with sharing common traditions, like a belief in one God, some people believe that their religion, or their God is the only God, and the most holy one, and everyone else practicing other religions, or believing in another God, or multiple gods, are completely wrong or sacrilegious. Ideally, it would be great if more people felt that there is truth or goodness in all religions, which is what we can hope for as we continue to evolve. This is why raising our consciousness is so very important. Religious, or "holy wars," which have been caused by "differences in religion," fill our history books. In history writer, Matthew White's book, The Great Big Book of Horrible Things, he cites religion as "the cause of 11 of the world's 100 deadliest atrocities."

As I said, this is not a book on religion. It is on how to practice Mindfulness so that we can be more awake, present, and aware, and in our awareness, we transcend limited thoughts and beliefs, especially the beliefs of those religions that pit us against one another, rather than embrace our differences with tolerance and compassion. By being more present, we are more aware of the thoughts we hold in our mind of ourselves and others no matter religious preferences or lack thereof. If you can do that, you stand a greater chance of experiencing the oneness that many people have felt during their mystical experiences, which seems to transcend beliefs or limited ideas of the mind. It is apparent from many of the mystical experiences that have been shared, that what was felt was a divine connection to something greater than the "self," and this is the divine I'm referring to when I say, living a divine life.

If you are open to living a life of heightened awareness, a state of mind that Jane Goodall felt she "slipped into," which caused her to experience "the moment of truth" that suddenly came upon her, then you are likely to experience more divinity in your life. This not only means "the state or quality of being divine" but also refers to a "fluffy, creamy candy (or fudge) made with stiffly beaten egg whites" (Merriam-Webster's Dictionary).

I am presenting to you words that are more commonly associated with religion, like divine, and mysticism, for you to fold into your daily lives. This, I believe, will make us feel that we can experience these higher states of consciousness, and that it isn't only accessible or reserved for holier, or more pious beings than us. If experiencing a higher state of consciousness was only possible for those who are devoutly religious, then God is only available to certain people doing certain things. I can't speak for God, but something tells me that isn't true. Each and every one of us is capable of "transcending animal instincts" and experiencing a "transcendental reality" if we connect to the divine within ourselves, whether it's through religion or the unexpected mystical experience you can have walking down a "squalid street" as Evelyn Underhill had. It doesn't matter how we connect to the divine, for that is solely personal. I don't care if you are devoutly religious, or you experience divinity eating creamy candy.

I am asking if you want to live a life with greater meaning, and maybe that greater meaning can happen if you raise your awareness a little more so that everything in your life can mean more to you than it does right now. Here are a few questions to ask yourself about your life presently:

1. What does your life mean to you?
2. Does your life hold deep meaning for you?
3. If "yes," what meaning does your life hold for you?
4. If "no," what meaning would you like your life to hold for you?
5. What does "divine" mean to you?
6. What would "living a divine life" mean or look like to you?
7. Do you want to live a divine life?
8. How can you begin to live a divine life?

It is the sovereign right of every human being to live their life exactly as their soul desires to. And if that means you simply want to be happy living your life following whomever you choose, or no one or nothing other than your heart, I embrace you. You must decide what brings you joy, and that might mean what Eleonora Duse says in this lovely quote:

"If the sight of the blue skies fills you with joy, if a blade of grass springing up in the fields has power to move you, if the simple things of nature have a message that you understand, rejoice, for your soul is alive."

It is a soul most alive that can live life more divinely. Do you wish to live this way? Begin each day allowing for your soul to show you the way to living a divine life, and be present so that you may listen to what it tells you.

I step upon the path of the divine

I ask that my soul guide me

So that I may live a divine life

I am present and ready to listen

MINDFULNESS & MYSTICISM

SELF-SURRENDER

When I let go of what I am,
I become what I might be.

— LAO TZU

Self-interest is but the survival of the animal in us.
Humanity only begins for man with self-surrender.

— HENRI FREDERIC AMIEL

Try something different, surrender.

— RUMI

What does it mean to surrender to our self? For me, it means to give up the fight, the fight to resist who we are, our most true, authentic self. And who might that authentic self be? Is it the self that is most known to us, or is it the self we have yet to know? Both. We have come to know ourselves up to this point, and now we continue our journey to know ourselves even more, and for that to happen, we must surrender to ourselves completely.

We can associate the word surrender to losing control, or feeling powerless, and this is what we must do to give into our vulnerability. When we let go of the need to control who we are, that is when, as Blaise Pascal, French physicist and theologian says, "All of our reasoning ends in surrender to feeling."

Surrendering to our self means we are not resisting what we feel, and no matter what it is we are feeling, we allow ourselves to feel it even more. I like to call this free-falling, which means being unafraid to plunge deeper into our heart and soul. We must trust that, just as a parachute opens when one is skydiving in mid-air, we will be caught and held in the embrace of protection. But first, you must jump, and that is the hardest part. Self-surrender is facing our greatest fears and saying, "I am ready to meet myself, all of myself, no parts left unknown," even if your fear makes you feel as though you can die.

And we can feel as if we are dying when we are ready to let go of the falseness that has buffered us from our true, raw, unguarded, unhidden, real, authentic self. We are letting go of the false self, which can feel like a death, but it is like the shedding of a skin a snake must do when a new skin is ready to grow, and when we look at the skin it has shed, it is dry and lifeless.

Whether we are aware of it or not, what we are yearning for is to surrender to something greater than the self that is familiar to us, even if we don't yet know what that is. It is in this act of surrendering that we bring ourselves to a divine power that awaits us, and we say to it, "I am ready to know you. I am ready to take you into myself. I am ready to become you." In essence, self-surrender is offering ourselves to the mystical, and declaring that there is nothing to fear there.

The mystical no longer needs to be hidden from us, or withheld, as if we are not worthy or deserving of it. We are all worthy and deserving of knowing the sacred truths of life, which is what true mystics are devoted to, but we must first strip ourselves bare of that which is not real, the false self or else the mystical cannot penetrate or enter us, even if we ask, or demand to be taken in by it. Terence McKenna, author, and modern-day mystic, has spoken of not expecting a mystical experience to "perform on demand" the way psychedelics do "because that would be essentially man ordering God at man's whim, which is not how it's supposed to work." No, we cannot order God at our whim, no more than we can order having a mystical experience. If we truly want to connect to something greater than who we think we must be in order to feel worthy or important, we must relinquish the false self that stands in the way of our readiness to receive a greater knowing of who we are, which is much more than our identity or persona. When we are connected to the divine, and let ourselves live it daily, the mystical will find its way to us, but we must surrender and keep surrendering until we are brought to our knees with humility and gratitude for this miraculous journey we are on.

We must continue to let go of the false self so that our most authentic self can keep us open and ready to receive the mystical experience, as I believe I was at a young age. I may have not yet known who my most authentic self was, as I was becoming the me that I am, and hope to continue "becoming" until my last breath, which I will talk more about in Being and Becoming. But when the pure essence of the soul is left alone to be, and rests in quietude and acceptance, that is when the mystical can visit us, when we do not resist our true soul essence, and are in a state of pure being.

Yes, the mystical experience is one each of us can have, but we can't demand or force it, for in our forcing, or insistence that we should experience euphoria, we hastily reach for the instant gratification of bliss and ecstasy, and that is when drugs, alcohol, or anything that gives us immediate gratification becomes a cheap replacement for union, connection and, ultimately, "oneness" which is the transcendence of self, and a connection to all that exists, visible and invisible. That is when we not only can experience the mystical, but we become "at one" with the mystical, for there is no separation from a Spiritual Consciousness, which I will also speak about more later.

So, basically, we must die first to a false self, and in this willingness to let go of all that isn't real, we birth a new self that is connected to all, but only through a type of surrender that does not fear death of a self with which we are so familiar. This may seem like asking a lot of ourselves, and we are, but if we are not willing to let go of everything that is false, nothing profound can come into our heart, unless we have emptied it completely of all that is not true and real.

Does that call to you? Does letting go of everything that is not real seem possible for you? And what does everything really mean? I mean, everything that you hold onto that tells you who you think you are, but aren't. And who do you think you are? Do you know? Do you know all of yourself? Or do you only want to know what pleases you, and makes you feel confident and important? Yes, you are important, but your importance does not mean what you have, or how popular you are, or how many people love you and tell you how great you are. No matter how important we think we are, we are ordinary. Not ordinary in a negative way, but ordinary in a way that gives us the opportunity to strive for more, and use our "ordinary powers," as Isaac Newton said, so that we can "apply it," and success can be achieved. But how do we want to do that?

If we apply our powers in such a way that gets us more of what we have, or makes us feel more successful having not surrendered to our authentic self, then we will only be successful at being untrue or false. We will sense this, and continue to desire more success for the wrong reasons. We already are extraordinary, and yes, we are also ordinary, which helps us aspire to become better and realize the depth of our extraordinariness. And where we can be the most extraordinary is when we have stripped ourselves bare of every morsel of falseness, and that is when we can shine as our most surrendered, radiant self. But, you must be willing to give up the self to which you have grown accustomed, especially if it is keeping you from loving the parts of yourself you find less lovable.

Self-surrender is asking you to face all of you. Every single aspect of you. Every flaw, every wrinkle, every fear, every insecurity, every lie. Can you do that? I know you can. And when you do, you will feel an inner knowing, a serenity, a truth; a truth that tells you that none of that is real. And this truth is part of the spiritual mystery of life. There are many sacred truths for us to realize on this mystical life journey, and as we surrender to our most authentic self, and keep surrendering in the days to come, more truths shall be revealed to us, and our divine light will be illumined even more.

I am surrendered

So that I may know

Divine Truth

I offer my false self

To be removed

Like a burden I did not ask for

I was born authentic

And I shall die authentic

MINDFULNESS & MYSTICISM

CHAPTER 8

BEING AND BECOMING

*They both listened silently to the water, which to them
was not just water, but the voice of life, the voice of
Being, the voice of perpetual Becoming.*

— HERMANN HESSE, SIDDHARTHA

*Being, not Doing, is the first aim of the mystic; and
hence should be the first interest of the student of
mysticism.*

— EVELYN UNDERHILL

Being and Becoming are happening to us simultaneously, but if we don't allow ourselves to emerge naturally, like the lotus does from muddy waters, we interrupt the process of becoming, which happens as it will. We must know that we are always in a constant flow of "perpetual Becoming" as Hermann Hesse said, and if we don't push, or force the delicate evolution of our being, we will become the ripened, wise version of ourselves when we are ready.

Mindfulness reminds us to be fully present in our being, no matter what stage of being we are in. It shows us in our awareness that where we are is exactly where we need to be, and we needn't do anything other than allow ourselves to free fall into the moment so that we can get what we need from it to learn and grow.

When we surrender to being real, as I spoke about in the previous chapter: Self-Surrender, and resist the false self, or any temptation we might have to hide who we are for fear of not being loved, we are aiding our becoming, as if we are midwifing the birth of our authentic self at every turn. This is the ebb and flow of our being/becoming, and what we begin to realize is that we are actually orchestrating our union with reality, which is the root, or the essence of the mystical experience. But we have more to learn before we think we can call upon this union without being fully conscious when we do it.

I consider the mystical experience a great privilege and not something we should assume we can have just because we are deserving of it, which we are. But if we don't value this life, and use and manipulate it to do what we want to continuously feed our ego, then we will keep expecting to be taken higher by something external, or outside of ourselves, when it is us that can "orchestrate our union with reality." This union will elude us unless we are committed to the integrity of our being and the development of our becoming.

The truth is, we want to be taken higher, plain and simple. We want to awaken each morning, not feeling the weight or burden of another day pressuring us to perform, or succeed, or win. So, we desire to be lifted from our frustration, sadness, loneliness, or misery, and the only way we know how to do this is to put something in us such as drugs or alcohol, or distract ourselves endlessly on social media, and it immediately makes us feel less pressure. Drugs and alcohol can lighten our mental load. They stimulate us, or relax us, or numb us. Whatever we need to feel, there is always something that can help us feel it. But what we are not using is the very thing that can lift us beyond the burdens of what we believe life imposes on us, and that's our natural gifts. We don't believe that we have the power to overcome life's difficulties, and how can we if we are disconnected from our being, the core essence of our soul and don't realize that all we need to do is go within the depths of our pure being to access the riches that are stored there.

Just as I spoke about the natural gifts of our brain, and the plethora of "feel-good" chemicals we can produce whenever we want to, we have completely ignored the miraculous creation that our being truly is. Do you realize what we have to work with? It is nothing short of remarkable! We may have "ordinary powers" that we must apply in order to realize what we are capable of, but if we were to really delve into the brilliance of our being, who we are, who we are becoming, and who we can continue to be we would find it is beyond mind-blowing!

Get to know your being, the true miracle that you are, and stay clear about who you want to continue becoming. If we keep ourselves awake, present, and aware of who we are, and everything around us, you can be sure that God, the Divine, the absolute, source, or whatever holds sacred or holy meaning for you will let its presence be known to you because you are letting your true presence be known to it. And that is when we are open to receive the mystical, and step into the "union with reality," for we are ready and unburdened by the illusions that tell us we are anything but divine in our being, which we are.

I am pure being

And in my pure being

I am becoming

Purer in my being

MINDFULNESS & MYSTICISM

CHAPTER 9

THE QUEST FOR SACRED TRUTHS

Three things cannot be long hidden:
the sun, the moon, and the truth.

— BUDDHA

The world is not what it appears to be.
Behind this surface life, where we experience the play of life
and death, there is a deeper life which knows no death; behind
our apparent consciousness, which gives us the knowledge of
objects and things...there is...pure...consciousness...Truth...
is experienced only by those who turn their gaze inward.

— SWAMI PRABHAVANADA

Oscar Wilde said, "The truth is rarely pure and never simple." I actually think that truth is essentially pure and simple, but we complicate it because that's what we do, we complicate things when we don't need to.

When something is too simple for us, we can make it more difficult for ourselves, and project our complexities onto people and things so they can be the reason for our suffering, and that's when we say, "It's complicated."

Yes, life can be complicated for sure, but it takes getting out of our own way, and out from under all of the drama we create constantly, to stop and look at the pure, simple beauty of something like a perfect rose, or the sunsets I am fond of talking about, or the smile of a loved one looking at us, or us at them. That is truth at its best. Truth is pure and simple, I believe, and if we don't recognize it as such, we miss its purity and simplicity. We blindly step out of the gift of a moment that brings us exquisite truth, and we foolishly think, "I need something more, something other than what is." What could that something be?

All of our wanting, and needing, and having, and then our wanting and needing to have more never seems to stop. We are endlessly on what I like to call the "hamster wheel," going 'round and round' in the never-ending samsara of our search, the cycle of life in the material world we are bound to, but what exactly are we in search of?

Is it the "miraculous" I spoke about in Chapter 2 -

Demystifying Mysticism, when I mention the title of Ouspensky's book, In Search of the Miraculous. Are we seeking something that can give us greater meaning in our lives, as I asked, and if so, what could that be? If we are not seeking the truth of our existence, then what is it we are constantly seeking? Don't we want to know what this life, this reality, truly is? It can't possibly be just what is on the surface, unless the surface is all you wish to know, and isn't that superficial?

Some people prefer living on the surface of life. The outer and the exterior is where they exist, which is like living outside of a magnificent palace. You may think you live within it, but you continue to live on what I call the exterior of the interior; for the interior is not the interior of the palace within you. You can live in the most beautiful, opulent palace, and live as a king or queen, but if you don't venture into the inner sanctum of your soul, and seek the true riches there, you will depend on material luxuries to satisfy you and will always seek for more to satiate your endless desire.

And that's what Buddha did. He was prince Siddhartha who had everything, and was given the name that means, "He who reaches his goal" and that he did. He chose not to follow in his father's footsteps as a king, but instead renounced his opulent home and family for the life of a seeker. He became a Buddha, an "enlightened being." The palace in which he grew up could not satisfy what he was seeking in his heart and soul, and that was knowing the truth of man's suffering. If the gilded walls of his family's palace could have provided true comfort for his soul, he would have stayed there. And that is what many of us do. We stay somewhere hoping that it will provide some comfort for our soul, but we neglect to look for something deeper than what is on the surface. We neglect to see beyond it, into the mystical.

The mystical is there. It is both on the surface and way beyond it, but we will miss it again and again because we don't set our gaze where we need to look. And when we look, we don't see as much as we can. If you only choose to look at the surface of things, and not be fully aware of what you see, as well as surrender to how you feel in your seeing, as I spoke about in Chapter 7 - Self-Surrender, then not only will you remain closed to the experience you are having, but the mystical will continue to elude you, and what a sublime experience you will miss.

Seek the truth, and you will venture on the path of the mystical, for it is where truth leads us. Truth takes us beyond anything we can imagine that exists only on the surface of life because the surface of life is only one layer of truth, and there are multitudes. The external is where it begins, like a doorway, and the mystical stands by, an invisible energy that waits for us to look at something, like the perfect rose. In our looking, and inhaling of its hypnotic fragrance, we stop, and do absolutely nothing other

than remain still and present in our pure being, and that
is how the mystical experience can happen, like an exalted
penetration. This is ultimate reality, the oneness that is
all. Call it God, call it the Divine, call it what you will. It
exists, and it is here for you, if you seek to know it.

This is what seeking the truth asks of us: to genuinely want to know it, and in our desire, we go beyond the
surface, for we know there is so much more for us to see
and know.

Ask yourself the following:

1. "Do I wish to seek the truth?"
2. "What is the truth I wish to seek?"
3. "Do I wish to seek only the surface of this life?"
4. "Can I look beyond the surface?"
5. "Am I ready to go beyond the surface?"
6. "Do I want to know the mystical?"
7. "Do I want to experience "union with reality?"

This "union with reality" that Evelyn Underhill called
the mystical experience is knowing the sacred truths of
this life, and they are only known to us if we seek to know
them. Not everyone lives this life as a seeker, and not everyone needs to seek more than they are able to know, or
handle. You needn't do more than acknowledge yourself
as a seeker of truth, and you will begin to see the truth

revealed to you in sometimes subtle, and other times very distinct ways. That is how the mystical works. It gives us hints, and clues, and signs, and we can either see them, or ignore them. Some people actually choose to ignore or deny things that are mysterious or inexplicable because the unknown is too frightening to go towards.

But the mystical experience is there waiting for you when you are ready to receive it, and it can come to you in many ways. It can appear to us in a dream with many messages and symbols. In some ancient societies, like Egypt and Greece, dreams were considered a type of supernatural communication. They could be interpreted as receiving divine messages one needed to get. Or, the mystical can come to us as a power animal, which is a shamanic belief that an animal comes to us as a spirit guide to protect us. Some people have claimed they felt something mystical when they unexpectedly encountered a coyote, which the Navajo believe "can come to warn you of something." The Shoshoni believe "the coyote symbolizes endings, which make way for new beginnings." When my brother Daniel passed away, I had so many mystical experiences with birds all around me. There was an owl outside my window that would repeatedly hoot in a very comforting way, as my heart broke over his passing. Interestingly enough, I always said that my brother was wise like an owl, and I felt with certainty that his spirit was communicating with me through the owl.

One night, when I sat outside in my backyard, the owl

flew out of the tree, swooped extremely low over my head, flew to another tree, then back to the tree it was in before and stayed there for several weeks after. A mystical experience? I have no doubt, but not everyone sees, or believes the mystical signs that are all around us. If we doubt, or fear it, unusual things can still happen to us, but we might not interpret them as "mystical."

Encountering numbers repeatedly is another way to feel connected to the mystical, and for people who explore it through numerology, they find that it often coincides with events happening in their life at the time, and it holds a particular spiritual meaning for them. The ancient Greek philosopher and mathematician, Pythagoras introduced the idea that all numbers have vibrational properties. Considered to be the "father of western astrology," he recognized that there was a spiritual and mystical side to numbers and held the belief that the numbers involved in the date of our birth, and the number of letters in our name, plays a great role in our destiny. I have always been aware of numbers in my life, and have ones that appear and reappear, which I consider very synchronistic.

Mine are 7 and 11, and sometimes 22, but lately 4 has been showing up more. There are many different interpretations of numbers and their symbolism or meaning. In Judaism, 4 is considered a mystical number meaning "wholeness." Another spiritual meaning of 4 is that it is the number of "being," and it "connects mind-body-spirit with the physical world." The biblical meaning, or "story" of the number 4 is that on the fourth day, God created the sun, moon, and the stars, so it represents "creation." There were 4 gospels who authored the life of Jesus; Matthew, Mark, John, and Luke, and there are 4 matriarchs who were the "mothers of the tribes of Israel;" Sarah, Rebecca, Rachel, and Leah. There are 4 questions asked at the Passover Seder, and 4 cups of wine, which represents the redemption of the Israelites from slavery under the Egyptians. As we know, there are four seasons, as well as four directions on the earth; North, South, West, and East. In the Tarot, which is a deck of cards with imagery and symbolism meant for spiritual lessons, the number 4 is known as the "emperor card," and is a "symbol of authority." What does the number 4 mean to me, and why is it showing up in my life more? I would say that all of the numbers that have shown up in my life, and continue to show up, mean something to me for different reasons, and I pay close attention because there hidden in them are wise and ancient interpretations going as far back to St. Augustine (354-430AD), who said that "Numbers are the universal language offered by the deity to humans as confirmation of the truth." I feel that they have mystical messages that I am meant to receive at that moment in time, and can interpret them with a deeper understanding of them, depending on how aware and ready I am to understand what is being presented to me by a divine source. The number 4 could mean something very specific and resonant to me today; and tomorrow, it could mean something entirely different that I am meant to know then. I say, let the numbers guide you, and use their meaning and symbolism wisely, but don't try and control where they might lead you because that too is part of the great mystery.

Mysticism constantly leads us towards mystery and wonder, and just when we think we have everything figured out, or understand things like numbers that appear in our life, a whole new truth can be revealed to us. All we need to do is be present and aware enough to fully understand that truth, and how it pertains to our life at that time. If numbers are a "confirmation of the truth" you need to get, or wish to receive, how wonderful is that!

Maybe you have numbers in your life that continue to appear, which hold a particular meaning for you. More and more people are talking about seeing the numbers 11:11 appearing around them either on clocks, their phone, license plates, addresses, or even bank statements. I am aware of it when it pops up on my phone, and since I feel resonant to the number 11, which according to numerology is considered a "master number" that signifies "intuition, insight" and even "enlightenment," I pay closer attention to it.

Some numerologists, psychics, or mediums explain the numbers 11:11 appearing out of nowhere as not just a coincidence, but an auspicious sign, and we should pay close attention to it because it is a message from the universe to become more conscious, aware, and be open to "experience a relationship with the divine."

I'm pleased that people are becoming more conscious and aware, and if seeing the numbers 11:11 is helping them do that, or reminding us to be more present in the moment, I consider it "Mindfulness meets mysticism," which is what this book is all about. But, even with these signs, we must still look beyond the "first layer of truth," as I have mentioned, meaning that even signs or symbols can be shrouded in mystery, and we must be even more aware to discern and interpret the messages we are receiving wisely. Know that the mystical path is like peeling a never-ending onion, and just when we have figured out one mystery, there are many more to uncover and solve.

Whatever it is you seek, seek it with a deep desire to know. You might encounter the mystical in ways, as I said, that can be subtle, or very distinct. However you experience the mystical, make sure to be as present and aware as you can so that you can really see, take in, and understand what it is you are experiencing. If you keep your mind open, and your thoughts illumined, truths will be known to you when you are ready to know them.

If you do seek the sacred truths of life, be patient in your seeking. Remember what I said: "you cannot force or demand that the mystical reveal itself to you, but when it does, you will know it." If you stay committed to seeking the truth, and remain awake, present, and aware in your commitment, I have no doubt that the mystical will make its presence known to you by how you make your presence, and quest for knowing the sacred truths of life, known to it.

Dear Sacred Truths of Life
I wish to know you
I seek you out
And will continue
Seeking you
For all the days to come
Until I know
Yes until I know

MINDFULNESS & MYSTICISM

CHAPTER 10

LIFTING THE VEILS

There was a door to which I found no key:
There was the veil through which I might not see.

— OMAR KHAYYAM

This is love: to fly toward a secret sky, to cause a hundred veils
to fall each moment. First to let go of life. Finally, to take a
step without feet.

— RUMI

I spoke about there being many layers of truth, and if we live life on the surface, we cannot see the greater truths that live beyond the external. The first layer is like a door, and we can either stand before it or refuse to enter it either because we either have no desire to, or believe we don't have the "key," as Omar Khayyam says in his quote above. But he also says, "There was the veil through which I might not see."

We can search for the key we think we need in order to walk through the door of truth, or we can know that it has no lock and instead many veils for us to lift. But we must see the veils in order to lift them, and there are many. The veils represent illusion, and we live this life surrounded by false ideas and beliefs, some of them others, and some of them our own. When we seek the truth, the veils of illusion fall away, and with each one that does, our consciousness is raised, and our own falseness is transformed into a greater knowing, which is that we are in "union with reality" and that reality is free of illusion.

This journey of awakening requires us to be a good veil lifter. If you, yourself, wear a veil of a false self, and haven't done the work of self-surrender I spoke about in Chapter 7, then you remain hidden to yourself and are choosing the path of self-deception, and that is about as far removed from your true nature as you possibly can be.

Our pain and suffering come from no other place than that we are living a lie, and that lie is a type of deception we hold onto because we believe (falsely) that we must live this way in order to be accepted or loved. That deep yearning we have to be loved can be so great, we will do anything we can to get that love, even if it means being who we are not, and suppressing our most authentic self, which is like forcibly putting an end to who we are. Picture, if you will, offering your false-self up like a piece of meat and letting others consume your falseness like genetically modified beef. I know that might be a very unpleasant image to imagine, but falseness of any kind is artificial, and what's more, it can be like a contagion. If we don't diligently lift the veils of falseness and illusion in ourselves, we spread falseness like a disease. Before you know it, we are living amongst one another infected by falseness, even a type of hollowness, which has spread like a plague.

This brings to mind an eerie quote by George Orwell from his novel 1984: "You will be hollow. We shall squeeze you empty, and then we shall fill you with ourselves."

Throughout history, many civilizations crumbled, and were destroyed because that plague, an infestation of falseness took over, and people were able to be "filled" with something other than who they were. It was dark and sinister. Nazi Germany is a perfect example of that. Were it not for the twisted, demonic falsehood that permeated an entire country, and spread like wildfire throughout Eastern Europe, the horrific untruth to hate, destroy, and savagely murder millions of innocent people could not have possibly happened. The veils of falsehood were there big time, and tragically, not enough people were good, or decent enough veil lifters, to stop it.

I've asked myself the following endless amounts of times: "Where was everyone?" They were there. Yes, they were there alright. Millions of people stood idly by because they, themselves, hid behind their own deceptive veils. They allowed the veils of illusion to be worn by others, and before anyone knew it, that contagion, that disease of falseness was everywhere, and the veils became so dark and black that no one could see the light anymore.

But, the light returned, because the light always does; however, if you're not careful, and the veils of deception begin to be the current trend again, well, we know that means the masquerade ball is upon us. You can either choose to come as your most true, authentic self, or instead allow self-deception to be your costume, which means falsehood is in full swing again. So be careful, very careful.

The metaphor of the masquerade ball is to illustrate a point of how dangerous deception, deceit, and dissimulation of any kind can be. An innocent masquerade ball can be quite fun because we dress up for a period of time, and then we remove our costumes when the ball is over.

Unfortunately, many people prefer their costume, which I'm referring to as the false-self, and have no desire

to remove it. There is a price to pay for living a lie, and if
you don't recognize it in yourself, or don't identify it when
you see it in someone else, and play along with that deception to keep an illusion going that you think is necessary or important, then the lie becomes a reality, and that
reality is not in union with anything other than deception.

Veil lifting is something we pretty much have to do
daily because there are so many veils around us. As I said,
some of them are ones we wear, and many of them are
not. If you live your life veil free, I commend you. That
is like being totally naked, and I don't mean disrobed. I
mean the type of naked that allows you to move through
life being honest, real, and completely undisguised, and
that is so damn attractive as far as I'm concerned. I love
realness. Always have, and always will. As a woman,
I know we can do things to adorn ourselves like wear
make-up, and do whatever enhancements we choose to
keep ourselves looking attractive, which men do, too. But
I am hearing more and more women say they want to
remove their breast implants, or let their hair grow out to
its natural color because they no longer want to be seen
or loved for someone they are not, and it takes courage to
do that. We all hide to varying degrees, and concealing, or
not revealing everything about ourselves can be thought
of as mysterious or alluring. I think that's fine if you're
not deceiving yourself, or someone else, and making sure
that choosing to conceal, or not reveal everything about

yourself all at once is because there is a type of divulging or disclosing that is like a courtship. We pace ourselves to share or reveal who we are, and might be more comfortable doing it incrementally.

And then, there are those people who are open books, and reveal who they are immediately. In whatever way you choose to reveal yourself, make sure that you lift any veils if you have them. When we speak honestly from our heart, and even tell someone that we are afraid to reveal who we really are, we might be surprised that they feel the same way too. As I said, revealing all of who we are takes courage because we are taking a chance of being judged, and even not loved for who we are. We do take a risk in revealing ourselves, but isn't that a risk worth taking? If we are not willing to lift the veils of the false-self, and instead mask or hide ourselves from being seen for who we truly are, then we can never know for sure why someone is attracted to us, or even loves us. That is why when people are so tired of being who they are not, and tell their family, friends, or partner the truth about themselves, it can be met with resentment and anger, as if you deliberately misled or deceived someone by being who you're not.

We must lift the veils of deception in order to know the truth, and if we wish to know it in all of its sacredness, we must be willing to remove falseness of any kind. As Shakespeare said so famously, "To thine own self be true," and it is most important that we live true to ourselves, first and foremost. Without living truthfully to ourselves, we cannot be true to anyone else. And, if we don't continue to lift the veils of deception, we agree to live dishonestly.

Stand at the door of truth, and know that you can enter it at any time. You not only hold the key, but you can see through the veils of falseness, if you so choose, and can remove yours too, if you find yourself wearing one. We are always asked to see more than we do, which requires us to look more deeply.

Ask yourself the following:

1. Do I wear a veil of falseness?
2. Am I willing to remove my veil of falseness?
3. Can I recognize a veil of falseness in another?
4. Am I willing to be honest when I see a veil of falseness?
5. Do I wish to reveal my most authentic self?
6. Do I wish to be loved as my most authentic self?
7. Do I wish to live my life veil free?

As philosopher Blaise Pascal said, "Truth is so obscure in these times, and falsehood so established, that, unless we love the truth, we cannot know it." Be someone who "loves the truth" so much that you are willing to live your life free from any veils of falsehood. You are far too magnificent to hide yourself. Let the veils "fall each moment" as Rumi said, for each moment is an opportunity to be awake, present, and aware in our realness so that we can raise our awareness to a more heightened state of consciousness. There is no need to conceal who you are, and the belief that one must do so is nothing more than an illusion. Dispel it, transform it, and rise above it! Let the world know you, and be proud of the you that is most real, your pure being. This is the beginning of the mystical, my friend. Get ready to live it.

I have hidden from myself

But I hide no more

There is no need

To conceal who I am

Look at me closely

And see I wear no veils

If you cannot see who I am

My most authentic self

Perhaps you too are veiled

MINDFULNESS & MYSTICISM

CHAPTER 11

THE SPIRITUAL SHIFT

We must break the evil habit of ignoring the spiritual.
We must shift our interest from the seen to the unseen.

— AIDEN WILSON TOZER

It is not the strongest or the most intelligent who will survive
but those who can best manage change.

— CHARLES DARWIN

I wrote an article in 2013 for the Huffington Post called, "The Spiritual Shift, Do You Feel It?" It's interesting how long ago I wrote it, and the spiritual shift is only getting greater. What I said was this: "There's a spiritual shift going on, and if you haven't felt it yet, you most likely will, unless you don't want to, and if that's the case, you're going to notice a lot of interesting changes happening on the planet that will let you know that the shift is occurring. But, here's the thing, once you notice these interesting changes, the shift will happen to you too because you'll suddenly be aware of it, and that's what it takes, awareness." I go on to say, "Now, if you haven't felt the spiritual shift yet, and want to know what it is in a nutshell, here it is, oneness."

Oneness, that special feeling many people have felt during their mystical experience, has been described as feeling connected to everything. There is no separation from the self, and all that exists. This is what Jane Goodall means when she says, about her mystical experience, that "the self was utterly absent: I and the chimpanzees, the earth and trees and air, seemed to merge, to become one with the spirit power of life itself," which she believes happened because she "slipped into a state of heightened awareness."

When you have an experience like this, you know that you have had a shift in perception. You suddenly see things in a way that cause you to look at life very differently. Author, and philosopher Aldous Huxley describes this when he says, "When we feel ourselves to be sole heirs of the universe, when the sea flows in our veins...and the stars are our jewels, when all things are perceived as infinite and holy."

All things can be perceived as "infinite and holy" when we have a shift in our perception, and that is when we can experience the type of feel-good chemicals, which our neurotransmitters can produce. Our brains are ripe to join the universe in its miraculous, ongoing shift, which it is, constantly. We can enhance those feel-good chemicals if we participate in life as if we are in a slow dance with the cosmos. And when we free fall into it, we can ride the wave of bliss and euphoria because oneness is quite the high. As I asked before, "Can we feel this natural high all the time?" I think we can, and maybe that is what a true state of enlightenment feels like, but we are refining our awareness and awakening more each day, so a full dose of enlightenment is unlikely at this point in our spiritual evolution. But, as we continue to awaken more, we realize we can tap into that feeling of oneness, that non-separateness we can feel in meditation, or glimpse in a mystical experience. It's there for us to feel when we want a boost of energy that lifts us up from the doldrums of everyday life. It sure does beat relying on drugs, alcohol, and the constant need for distraction on our devices to do it for us.

The universe is always in its own state of being and

becoming, as are we, and is changing and shifting constantly. We may not see these changes because they aren't always visible to the eye, but when we are awake, present, and aware, and more attuned to all that exists around us, we can more easily shift into a higher state of consciousness, feeling the oneness, or "union with reality" because we recognize we are not separate from it, and that knowing can feel euphoric.

A spiritual shift means there is a shift in consciousness, and our consciousness is always shifting. The key is to be aware of the shifts in our consciousness, which Mindfulness helps us do. By doing so, we become much more aware, again, of our non-separateness from the universe. Essentially, we are riding the wave of the shift that is always occurring, and can feel sparks of divine energy along the way. All we have to do is pretty much tap into this divine movement of the universe and know that we are a part of it. And how do you do this?

Here is a visualization meditation to feel yourself connected to the spiritual shift that is constant.

1. Close your eyes.
2. Imagine yourself sitting on top of a white, fluffy cloud.
3. Extend your hand out, and imagine it being touched by God, or a Divine presence (similar to Michelangelo's The Creation of Adam).
4. Feel yourself receiving a holy transmission.
5. Imagine it moving through your entire body.
6. Imagine yourself being filled with white light.
7. Imagine this white light moving up from the soles of your feet, and permeating out from the crown of your head.

Yes, there is indeed a spiritual shift happening, and whether you feel it or not, is okay. But, you can if you want to. If you practice Mindfulness, stay in present moment awareness, commit to self-surrender, and lift the veils of falsehood, I am certain you will feel the shift. You owe it to yourself to feel it because you are an important part of it. Your shift in consciousness helps raise consciousness higher on the planet. I would imagine you want to be a part of that, don't you? I hope so.

Stay present, be open, and dance. Dance slowly with the cosmos, and free fall into the bliss of surrendering. You are getting closer to the mystical more and more. I am excited for you and what waits ahead!

I free fall

Into the cosmic dance

I am part of the

Spiritual Shift that is constant

The mystical

Awaits me

MINDFULNESS & MYSTICISM

STATES OF CONSCIOUSNESS

*The key to growth is the introduction of higher
dimensions of consciousness into our awareness.*

— LAO TZU

*No problem can be solved from the same level
of consciousness that created it.*

— ALBERT EINSTEIN

*The ordinary waking consciousness is a very useful and, on
most occasions, an indispensable state of mind; but it is by no
means the only form of consciousness, nor in all circumstances
the best. Insofar as he transcends his ordinary self and his
ordinary mode of awareness, the mystic is able to enlarge his
vision, to look more deeply into the unfathomable miracle of
existence.*

— ALDOUS HUXLEY

If we looked at consciousness as states in a country, there are many. And, if we multiplied that by states in other countries, well, it seems vast, maybe endless. This can be said about consciousness. There are many states, meaning levels of awareness our consciousness can be functioning on, and how awake and aware we are of ourselves, other people, and our environment determines our present state of consciousness.

As I said in Chapter 3 - Awaken Now, "Being awake means how aware you are in all that you do. You may be alive, but that does not mean you are awake, consciously. That chapter explained how Mindfulness, which is being in the present moment with total awareness, helps keep us conscious, but, as we know, total awareness is different for each of us.

My total awareness might mean that I can intuitively pick up what someone is feeling before they even speak of it and help them in a moment of need. Or, it can mean that I see beyond someone's false self, into their soul, and by mirroring their authentic-self back to them in my eyes, it disarms them. Or, it can mean that by taking my spiritual pulse, I know exactly what my soul yearns for, and live my life consciously, moment by moment, soul-driven. I can go on and on about how we can live our lives with total awareness, or, at least, more awareness than we usually bring to a moment. As I said, staying present is a challenge, but if we are committed to practicing Mindfulness, and pay close attention to the nudges, pushes, or even shoves we can get when we step out of a moment, as I also spoke about in Chapter 3 -

Awaken Now, then we are diligently working on our states of consciousness, and they can be raised incrementally.

The goal, if you wish for it, is to reach higher states of consciousness so a mystical experience can become more natural for us. This doesn't only have to be something mystics can realize. But, here's the thing about mystics: they seek to obtain unity with the Divine, be it God, or a Divine presence that is personal so that spiritual truths can be known beyond the intellect. They are committed to the mystical path every step of the way, and mind you, it isn't always a bed of roses. Please be warned that this isn't some whimsical desire, or spiritual bypassing for your journey of awakening. There is far too much bragging of awakening these days, as far as I'm concerned. And about the slang word "woke," which means, "I was sleeping, but now I am woke," all I can say about that is this: how woke do you think you really are? Are you woke enough to know that you might not be woke enough, and if you're not woke enough, how do you think you're going to become more woke?

Spiritual awakening is serious business, and if you want to practice it daily, you might want to consider taking the Raise Your Consciousness Challenge, which I wrote about in my book, Live True. This means that everything you do, every word you say, every action you take is meant to raise your consciousness, and that is going to keep you mighty busy in the consciousness department.

Waking up happens gradually, and again, the more committed we are to being present and aware, the more awake we become, hence the more conscious we are.

We must remember that Buddha didn't just awaken and become enlightened all at once. He was on a path of awakening. And when I think of Siddhartha Gautama, who became a Buddha, which means a person who has attained Buddhahood and becomes an "awakened one" his path was probably more arduous and painful than we can imagine. I picture his inner journey being one of exploring both the light and dark aspects of the psyche, as if he went into his mind and performed surgery, thought by thought, to cleanse his mind of wrong thinking, and dispel the false self. I'm talking serious self-surrender to lift the veils of illusion!

Does this interest you? I'd be lying if I said that raising our consciousness isn't hard work. It is. This means that every moment of our life in which we are awake, we can actually be more awake than we are, if we choose to. You might not want that, and if that's the case, that's fine. Maybe you're perfectly happy being as awake as you are, but let me ask you this: Don't you want to experience more heightened awareness, and a type of euphoria or bliss that can happen when you're in a more heightened state of awareness? You, yourself, can make that happen without any drug or stimulant other than your own mind, which I spoke about in Chapter 3 - Awaken Now. Mystical moments can come upon us, but only if we are present enough for them to happen. And this union, this oneness, this unity consciousness that we can experience is worth every single effort we've put into heightening our awareness and raising our consciousness.

I want you to be aware of the different states of consciousness so you can gauge your own awakening. Although there are many, and, as I said, levels of awareness are purely subjective, let's focus on the states of consciousness that are in our range of possibilities so we may realize each one as we inch our way to higher states of consciousness. From a psychological perspective, psychologist Sigmund Freud believed there are three levels of consciousness:

1. Conscious – The part of the mind that holds what you're aware of.
2. Preconscious – The part of the mind where ordinary memory is stored.
3. Unconscious – The part of the mind not directly accessible to awareness.

I think it's good to know the different parts of our mind where consciousness functions, but this book is not going to focus too much on the psychological aspects of consciousness. We are going to focus more on the spiritual understanding of how Mindfulness plays a crucial role in awakening. By heightening our awareness and raising our consciousness, we can live a more mystical life, which again is being in union with the reality of non-separateness also called oneness, or unity consciousness.

From a Transcendental Meditation perspective, there are levels of consciousness that make up the path of spiritual development. They are as follows:

1. Waking consciousness – The state of consciousness you experience when you are awake and aware of your thoughts, feelings, and perceptions.
2. Sleep consciousness – The state of waking consciousness paused or turned off when not dreaming.
3. Dreaming consciousness – The transition into a dream state from waking consciousness.
4. Transcendental consciousness – The state of consciousness after waking, sleeping, and dreaming states. It is described as wakeful, alert, and conscious of self.
5. Cosmic consciousness – The state of a higher form of consciousness than that possessed by the ordinary man.
6. God consciousness – The consciousness of a higher self, transcendental reality, or God.
7. Unity consciousness – The state of consciousness that unites us to ourselves, others, nature, or the God of our understanding.

The first three levels of consciousness are experienced by every human being with a functioning nervous system, and the last four levels are thought to become accessible only as one meditates on a regular basis. Again, this is a theory based on the practice of Transcendental Meditation, which is a technique derived from the ancient Vedic tradition of India by Maharishi Mahesh Yogi for "avoiding distracting thoughts and promoting a state of relaxed awareness."

As a meditator myself for over thirty years, I cannot extol the benefits of it enough. If I could pin point one of its most invaluable advantages, it would be that of self-observation, and transcending the concept of "self." Going back to Transcendental Meditation, that is the fifth level of awareness called "cosmic consciousness," which is "going beyond the small me," and can also be called, "witness consciousness."

As much as meditation, when practiced consistently, can drop us into an understanding of the self, and our non-separation of oneness, or unity consciousness, it's staying in that state of awareness that is most challenging. This is why I believe that living a mystical life, and seeing everything through the lens of being in union with the reality that there is no separation from God, or a Divine presence, we move through life with an awareness that the "small me" isn't in charge. That means that when one walks down a squalid street as Evelyn Underhill did, and

experiences "indescribable beauty," or "joy and astonishment," it is not the "small self" that is the seer but something much greater than the self we know.

States of consciousness are, as I said, like states in
a country. We can visit them, but we don't necessarily
live there. And that's what we need to consider. Do we
want to just visit these states of awareness, or do we want
to spend quality time there? This is what we must ask
ourselves. The most important state of consciousness is
when we are awake. This doesn't mean we are fully aware,
nor does it mean that we are conscious in all that we do
while we are in an awake state. But it definitely is the
state we should pay the closest attention to, and work
the hardest on trying to raise our awareness in. Be aware
of how you spend your awake moments, and if you find
yourself stepping out of a moment, be your own Mindfulness guide. Give yourself a nudge, push, or even a shove to
keep yourself as awake, present, and aware as you possibly
can be. Remember, your "small self" is not running the
show, so don't let it. Aspire to heighten your awareness,
raise your consciousness, and hope that you are fortunate
to continue on the path of spiritual development with the
veils of falseness lifting one by one. As they do, you will
find yourself experiencing different states of consciousness
when you are ready.

My states of consciousness

Vary as I awaken

And in my awakening

I am more aware

Of the state of consciousness

I am in

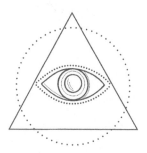

MINDFULNESS & MYSTICISM

HIGHER CONSCIOUSNESS

You are an explorer, and you represent our species, and the greatest good you can do is to bring back a new idea, because our world is endangered by the absence of good ideas. Our world is in crisis because of the absence of consciousness.

— LAO TZU

Consciousness is only possible through change; change is only possible through movement.

— ALDOUS HUXLEY

I've spoken about the different states of consciousness, and when we are in a higher state of consciousness, we are more open to having a mystical experience. And, when we practice Mindfulness, and are in present moment awareness, we are able to raise our awareness to such levels that we can feel as if our consciousness is like an ever-flowing stream in our awakening. So, in essence,

I'm saying that all of this is the perfect recipe for our consciousness to reign supreme. However, nothing can get heightened, if we, ourselves, are not in an active state of awareness, as I talked about in the previous chapter.

I'd like to tell you that heightened awareness happens pretty much on its own, and it can, but only if you're one of those people who is actively aware of your levels of awareness. That means, when it's waning, you know it, or, as I said, when you are half-asleep, you are fully aware that you are, and immediately wake yourself up.

In Zen Buddhism, there is something called "the Keisaku," which is a flat, wooden stick that is used during meditation by a teacher or master to strike the student's back when they are sleepy, or have lapses of concentration. It can cause a momentary sting, and may seem harsh or brutal. In actuality, it's not considered a punishment, but a "compassionate means to reinvigorate and awaken the meditator who may be tired from many sessions of Zazen," which is a meditative practice in the Zen Buddhist tradition. The whole purpose is to stop the "monkey mind," which is a Buddhist term for being in a mental state that is overwhelmed with thoughts.

This may sound like mental calisthenics, and it is, of sorts, but if you're not wanting to take control of your mind and make sure it's in tip-top shape, which means you're aware of the monkey mind, and practicing thought illumination (you've been keeping those thoughts positive, and full of light, right?), then, unfortunately, your awareness can diminish. You then run the risk of falling into the "not awake enough" category, and experiencing higher states of consciousness is not going to happen.

I know, this seems like a lot of work, or as someone once said to me, "It takes so much work to be self-aware." It most certainly does, but it's work that not only keeps your mind totally awake and alert, but this type of sharp awareness can also take you to such heights, you might feel like you're in a euphoric state of consciousness. You may feel as if your spirit is soaring out of your body, dancing with the cosmos. You and the cosmos are having a love affair that, well, why don't I let your very awake, and imaginative mind take it from there, if or when you get there.

You can, as poet John Milton said, "Trip the light fantastic," when you're in a heightened state of consciousness, and that means, "to dance, in an imaginative or fantastic manner." This is the absolute beauty of being in a state of heightened awareness. You are the arbiter of the levels of your consciousness, and walk that lovely, delicate line of orchestrating your union with reality, dipping into oneness whenever you feel like it. Don't get me wrong, I'm not saying we can "demand" a mystical experience, but we certainly can ease ourselves into the spiritual mystery of life by being ready, and ready means open and available to be "energized by the invisible," as Evelyn Underhill said.

I know, this might sound so esoteric, or for some people, "out there." But, what I want to ask you is, "Where is out there?" Is out there a place that only the stars can occupy, and if that's the case, aren't we "made of star stuff," as Carl Sagan said so beautifully? That means the "carbon, nitrogen, oxygen, and atoms in our bodies were created in previous generations of stars over 4.5 billion years ago," as he also said; so, yes, we are "out there" for sure.

All of life is mystical. The universe, the cosmos, and us. We are about as mystical as it gets, but we don't even know how mystical we are because our awareness is nowhere near as heightened as it can be. We can definitely live life in a more heightened state of awareness, which is absolutely possible for us. If we diligently practice Mindfulness, which simply requires us to be fully present and aware in the moment, it will increase and heighten our awareness daily. But we can barely do that because half the time we're so busy being busy, we hardly make room for our awareness to heighten. You've got to stop, and I mean really stop, if you want your awareness to increase. You can't constantly be busy on your devices, or running from pillar to post trying to reach some kind of eureka moment because what you will end up doing is chasing that type of joyous moment over and over again, and not realizing it. Here's the thing. The eureka moment isn't something over "there." Your cry of joy will happen when you realize that all of it is within you. As Rumi said so simply, "What you seek is seeking you." So, what's with us running around like chickens without a head so much of the time?

What are we doing? Do we not know that what we are truly seeking is this oneness, this wholeness, this non-separation of self from all that exists, but think instead that it's somewhere on the screens of our devices we keep scrolling on, and where will all of this scrolling end? It certainly isn't going to heighten our awareness, or raise our consciousness in a spiritual way, unless we realize in all of our scrolling that it's actually bombarding our senses with too much stimulation and assaulting our consciousness with sensory overload. If we don't put an end to our obsessive need to be busy and distracted constantly, we will remain at the mercy of something that clearly isn't raising anything other than our adrenalin levels and heart rate. This is not the type of raising of consciousness that can serve us best, and Terence McKenna is absolutely right when he says: "our world is in crisis because of the absence of consciousness." What do we want to do about it?

I don't mean to dangle the mystical experience in front of you like a carrot and what a spectacular carrot it is. But you don't really think you can snap your fingers and make it happen if you're too busy engaging in so many external activities and distractions, do you? The mystical experience can't happen if you're so busy focusing on yourself, or the "small self," it can't step in and court you. Think of it as the most exquisite manifestation of a human being who really wants to dance with you, but you're not even open to the mystical in human form stepping in. You see, mysticism takes shape in many forms, even though it has been described mostly as something invisible. But the invisible can become very visible, like a spirit animal, which I spoke about in Chapter 9 - The Quest for Sacred Truth. The mystical is always there waiting for you, as I said, when you are ready to receive it, and it can come to you in many ways.

But if we aren't heightening our awareness, which helps raise our consciousness, there is much of the mystical we miss. When I speak about the type of sharp awareness that can take you to such heights that makes you feel like your spirit is soaring out of your body, and dancing with the cosmos, I'm talking about a very special kind of dance. That means you have asked the mystical to dance with you, and if you're doing that, you're most likely in a heightened state of awareness to be able to do it. But, again, in order for that to happen, you must be present, very present.

You cannot be in the cosmic dance of life unless you are totally present, so I suggest you keep on staying as present as you possibly can. And, in your present moment awareness, you can raise your consciousness incrementally, and by raising it steadily, you are saying "yes" to the mystical. It will find you and dance with you like you've never been danced with before because it knows how much you want to, and how ready you are for that to happen.

Dance with me mystical

I am ready for you

In my heightened state of awareness

We shall "trip the light fantastic"

You and I

Yes we will dance

And the stars will clap for us

Each and every one of them

MINDFULNESS & MYSTICISM

CHAPTER 14

THE COSMIC DANCE

We ought to dance with rapture that we might be alive...
and part of the living, incarnate cosmos.

— D. H. LAWRENCE

Every child has known God,
Not the God of names,
Not the God of don'ts,
Not the God who ever does anything weird,
But the God who knows only four words.
And keeps repeating them, saying:
'Come dance with me, come dance.'

— HAFIZ
(translation by Daniel Ladinsky)

Human beings, vegetables, or cosmic dust, we all dance to a
mysterious tune intoned in the distance by an invisible player.

— ALBERT EINSTEIN

Are you dancing yet? I mean the cosmic dance. That's free-falling into your most authentic self, and in your total self-surrender, you are ready, as Milton said, to "trip the light fantastic." That's the kind of dancing I'm talking about.

The cosmic dance is dancing with "rapture," as D.H. Lawrence suggests we do, and that's when we live like the cosmos in human form. We are spiritual beings, lest we forget, so we must be mindful not to fall into the traps of the mundane. This fails to inspire our spirit to dance and makes us feel that the cosmic dance is something that seems so, well, out there. Guess what? We are out there!

How can you paint the Sistine Chapel, like Michelangelo; or write Beethoven's Symphony No. 9 in D minor; or come up with Einstein's Theory of Relativity; or develop a motor that can run on alternating current, like Nicola Tesla had; or discover radioactivity, like Madam Curie, unless you are out there meaning you stepped outside the box of traditional, everyday thinking and created something different from anyone else? Remember what I said in Chapter 4 - Transcending the Ordinary: "What is most average about people who think they're ordinary are their thoughts, and that can change at any time." I also said: "If you think you're ordinary, and deserve what seems befitting of an ordinary person, then that is what you will manifest for yourself." And, if that's the case, you're not making room in your mind to think thoughts that maybe nobody else has, and who knows what interesting, creative, or even fascinating things you might think up.

If you're someone who doesn't think outside the box, feels uncomfortable going towards the unknown, has an aversion to trying anything new or different, let alone exotic, and basically, don't like to be out of your comfort zone in any way, then the cosmic dance might not be for you. But, even if you are the kind of person I just described, and you've gotten this far in my book, and you haven't been uncomfortable with anything I've said thus far, then I believe you're a perfect candidate to experience the cosmic dance. Let me explain more of it to you so you won't think that you have to be an "out there" weirdo to do it.

There's something called the cosmic dance of Shiva, a Hindu God known as "the destroyer or transformer." Shiva symbolizes the interplay of both a "divine and static energy flow that contains the five principals of eternal energy: creation, preservation, destruction, illusion, and emancipation." He is the symbol of "universal consciousness" and considered the destroyer God because he removes evil from the world.

This is quite a cosmic dance Lord Shiva orchestrates to keep balance in the world, and when I talk about "orchestrating our own union with reality," I pretty much mean that we, too, are balancing a flow of energies that are both "divine and static." Those five principals of "eternal energy, creation, preservation, destruction, illusion, and emancipation" are energies we must navigate all around us. Even though we don't have a job as huge as Lord Shiva, which is to "remove evil from the world," we have no small role on this great big planet, and are also symbols of "universal consciousness" by how we raise our own.

Our consciousness is connected to the collective, or "universal," which brings us back to "oneness," also referred to as "unity consciousness." Basically, it means that we are all connected as one unified stream of consciousness, and each of us has a very important role in the universe. Whether we think we are a cosmic dancer or not, the truth is we are all dancing in the cosmic dance of life, and we also play a role in removing "evil from the world" if you are led by the light.

If we don't think that who we are, what we think, how we behave, and what we do affects the "universal consciousness" of this planet, then yes, maybe we aren't "out there" connecting in a divine, cosmic way. But what we are is "out of touch," and that means out of touch with reality, the reality that is most real, not some made up story or narrative we've drummed up to keep our egos pumped up, and our illusions in place so that we can continue wreaking havoc on this poor planet Earth, and what has the great Mother Earth ever done to us? Wake up, dear friends, wake up. It is time right now. Not a single moment more can be wasted.

So, would you rather be out there in a divine, cosmic way, connected to yourself, others, nature, and to a God or

Divine source of your understanding, or would you prefer
being out of touch and very removed from anything that
is divine or cosmic? If so, I hate to tell you, but you are
out of touch with reality. That means you are not in union
with God, or a Divine source, and whether you believe in
God or not, you are not living in a Godly or spiritual way.

I believe we want to live more consciously because we
are all cosmic dancers in this mystical creation called life,
and we are part of the infinite movement of the universe.
Remember, it, too, is being and becoming, just as we are,
and if you stay present and committed to heightening
your awareness, and raising your consciousness as much
as you possibly can, you can turn into quite an excellent
cosmic dancer, I'm sure. Would you like to get a sense of
what being a cosmic dancer feels like?

Let me guide you.

1. Find a place where you can be alone. A room where you can comfortably move about, or outdoors in nature.
2. If you want, put on some music that you like.
3. Take a few deep breaths in and out.
4. Take a few moments to connect to a place in your body that feels vital or sensual.
5. Imagine tremendous light, heat, and power coming from that place.
6. Begin to move your body, letting that energy guide you.
7. Allow yourself to transcend thought, and imagine you are guiding the universe in a motion that feels free and uninhibited.
8. Feel your power, your strength, your freedom.
9. Surrender to the movement of your body, going deeper into your dance.
10. Let it guide you, surprise you, delight you.
11. Think of yourself as a God or Goddess of the universe, spreading your love and light everywhere.

The feeling you can experience when you let yourself
go into a deep trance of bodily freedom, and allow for
nothing to radiate from you other than love and light,
is a type of cosmic dancing. Whether you are actually
dancing, or moving through life doing your daily activities
like talking, eating, working, and all of the things we do
every day, and participating in life as our most authentic
self we are in the flow of universal consciousness. We are
not "out of touch" with the divine, but instead completely
aligned with it. When we do that, we not only are open
to a mystical experience, but we are in a prepared state
to experience oneness. You see, oneness is being in union
with reality, a reality where all veils of falseness have been
lifted, but that doesn't mean we have to only be sitting
in meditation to realize it. We can shift into oneness
wherever we are, but the key is learning how to navigate
the mystical with everyday life so we can move through
it more seamlessly feeling more at one with everything
around us, than not. This takes practice and refining the
art of being and becoming. We rest more in being with
acceptance, and are non-resistant in our constant transi-
tions of becoming.

You are a cosmic dancer, as we all are, for we live
amongst the cosmos, and as Carl Sagan says, "we are
made of star stuff." We are Buddhas in the making. Yes,
we have Buddha-nature within us, the inherent nature
to become enlightened, but we must learn how to tran-

scend the limitations of our mind so that we can be in a state called "Luminous Mind," which is a Buddhist term that means a "mind of clear light," or a "brightly shining mind," which divine thought illumination helps us realize. Thinking that you are a cosmic dancer, and allowing yourself to dance like one, is being in a state of the luminous mind. Be present. And, when life pulls you into Maya, which means illusion, and makes you feel that you have to participate in the falseness that isn't you, picture yourself lifting the veils of the inauthentic self, and imagine free-falling into a cosmic dance with life, which you are in, always.

I am in a cosmic dance with life

Each thought I have

Each word I say

Each action I take

Is part of the cosmic dance

MINDFULNESS & MYSTICISM

CHAPTER 15

INTELLIGENT BEINGS

I believe alien life is quite common in the universe,
although intelligent life is less so.
Some say it has yet to appear on planet Earth.

— STEPHEN HAWKING

Human beings are supposed to be the smartest
species on Earth. We are pretty damn intelligent,
and have accomplished many brilliant things, for
sure, but we have also done some of the stupidest
things too, which makes other species seem far more
intelligent than us sometimes. If intelligence is rated
by how well a species performs the job of being a
successful member of that species, then dolphins, who
don't have to manipulate their environment like we
do to survive, and get to focus their intellect on other
things, could possibly be more intelligent than us.

I have always been very drawn to dolphins, and they seem very intelligent to me. They also seem conscious, a lot more conscious than a large percentage of human beings, with whom we share this planet with. If intelligence were rated on consciousness, I'm afraid we would fail terribly.

In the days of the hunter-gatherer, approximately two million years ago, man had to kill animals for their food to survive. Survival was their main, if not only, modus operandi, or "habitual way of operating," and they did a really good job of it. So back then, we would be considered extremely intelligent, way more intelligent than any other animal alive at that time. The hunter-gatherer also harnessed the use of fire, became very knowledgeable of plant life, and developed their own technology for hunting and "domestic purposes." It seems to me they were very intelligent, indeed!

We've come a long way since this prehistoric group of nomads, have we not, and the type of "foraging," or searching for food, we do today is quite different. We have apps for that, and all we have to do is pick one of the many food delivery services to bring us what we want to eat in the privacy and safety of our own home. No saber tooth tigers to worry about there!

Ah, the 21st century. What a remarkable time to be alive in, but also a concerning one. Man has advanced beyond hunting for domestic purposes. Hunting today is considered a sport which I believe is a savage one, especially animals that are being hunted to extinction. Estimates say that by mid 21st century 30% of species may be extinct. Not a whole lot of consciousness being raised by those people who do it, I'm afraid, and the only type of mystical experiences they probably have is being at one with their brutal act of killing, which is barbaric and anything but conscious.

In some tribal communities, hunting for food is still done, for it is their only way to eat and survive. And for others who like to do something like fish for food, not because their survival depends on it, but because it's enjoyable for them, the bigger the fish you catch, the more praise you get. That goes for the size of elk antlers men still put in their man caves. Size matters to the modern man, does it not?

When we're not killing one another, either in wars or some type of hate crime, or slaughtering animals that are quickly becoming extinct, we're advancing intelligence, and have even created something called "Artificial Intelligence" (A.I.), which is also called "machine intelligence." This is a type of intelligence that is "demonstrated by machines," and compared to the "natural intelligence" humans and other animals have. I guess our natural intelligence is so in need of advancement that machines are the only ones fit for the job. I'm waiting for the day we get outsmarted by a machine, and don't know how to outsmart the very thing we created to outsmart us. I guess we'll have to ask Artificial Intelligence to guide us in how to reclaim our intelligence because we seem to be giving it away right and left to every inanimate object we're creating.

And, yet, the one area that is in the greatest need of advancing is our consciousness, and as I've spoken about in Chapter 3 - Awaken Now, being awake means how aware you are in all that you do. You may be alive, but that does not mean you are awake, consciously. I also said that being awake consciously means that you are fully present, and being fully present means you are consciously aware of how present you are. I finalize my point by saying we can be awake doing, but if we are not fully aware of who we are in our doing, and how conscious we are doing whatever we are engaged in, then we're just not awake enough. And we're not. Too many people fall into the category of "not awake enough," and I don't know about you, but I find that very troubling. How can we strive to create a type of artificial intelligence that's supposed to simulate and mimic our own, but we haven't spent as much time and effort developing a sharper awareness of the seriousness of what we're creating? Creating these types of intelligent machines that work and react like humans is very serious business, and if we're not careful, and make sure we are in a constant state of heightened awareness about this, these machines could potentially outsmart us and be our undoing. Are we not aware that we could be contributing to the most dangerous level of unconsciousness there is, and that's not acknowledging the consequences that might await us for what we are creating, and putting out into the universe?

This is called ignorance, which is not only the very opposite of intelligence, but also the lack of true knowledge. There is no greater knowledge than being in union with reality, and that reality is that if we are not conscious of how we are playing God, we will destroy ourselves. Yes, we are Godly, but that doesn't mean we always act intelligently, and to quote Einstein, "God does not play dice with the universe." So why should we? Who are we to place such little value on things like heightening our awareness, or raising our consciousness? We are so quick to view these aspirations as alternative or new age concepts, and not steeped enough in religion, or backed by science-based facts. Heightening awareness, and raising consciousness is what enlightenment is about. Is a machine that has been created to replicate us capable of that?

To quote Einstein again, because I feel you can't quote such a brilliant mind enough, "Only two things are infinite, the universe and human stupidity, and I'm not sure about the former." We keep trying to figure out the universe through science, and not delve deeper into understanding the mystery of consciousness, of which we are a part. We must understand ourselves, and know who we are, who we really are. Will Artificial Intelligence reveal that to us? Will machines tell us who we are? We might be able to create machines that can duplicate our intelligence, but, they have no awareness of who or what they are, and soon, in the not too distant future we may very well rely on them to tell us who we are because we ourselves will have forgotten.

And who are we really? Has the forgetting already begun? I think it has, which is why it is so crucial for us to awaken now. Be present. Lift the veils of falseness. And do not escape or rely on external things like drugs, alcohol or anything to numb you or get you so high you could die. Stick around if you'd like to see how this great cosmic mystery will unfold.

We can create machines that do all sorts of intelligent things, and can transport us to other places, but, there is no more mystical place than the one we can take ourselves to, and that is within our own soul. I don't have a problem with creating advanced technology and machines that can help us solve certain computer science problems, or transport us to other planets where human life might exist like ours. That is inevitable. Being "out there," and thinking more expansively will help us manifest our visions, just like the great visionaries I mentioned earlier. May we continue to think outside the box, but let's make sure that we're not creating a virtual box for ourselves, one that confines us to believe we are omnipotent, and can surpass God, Divine nature, or anima mundi, the world soul. Can we? We are part of the collective, the universe, the cosmos, the oneness, and the supreme consciousness that breathes life into us. Let us be aligned with it, and not try and control it or think we can outsmart it.

My intelligence
Is determined by
What I understand
And what I understand
Defines my intelligence
Let me know more than I do
And let what I know be
Steeped in true wisdom

MINDFULNESS & MYSTICISM

THE HUMAN SPIRIT

The human spirit must prevail over technology.

— ALBERT EINSTEIN

The body is only an instrument for the spirit.

— RUMI

Food for the body is not enough.
There must be food for the soul.

— DOROTHY DAY

The human spirit is defined as the spiritual or mental part of humanity, which makes up for a lot of what keeps our humanity going. Pierre Teilhard de Chardin said, "We are spiritual beings having a human experience," and it's very easy for our spirit to get taken over by the type of human experiences we are having.

We can get so caught up in what our human experiences ask and demand of us that our spirit can be pushed aside, or completely ignored, and before we know it something feels terribly wrong inside. We don't realize that we haven't been taking care of our spirit, and we pay a serious price for it.

When we feel a type of emptiness, or ennui, that's our spirit telling us something, something extremely important. But, far too often, people don't diagnose themselves properly, and instead of going deeper within to find out what's troubling them, they anesthetize themselves, or choose any type of distraction, and there are many, instead of tending to their spirit.

Think of the spirit as the wind that propels a boat to sail. Our spirit is what drives us, and moves us through life with vitality. If our spirit isn't being fed and nurtured, we can feel lethargic, unmotivated, and even depressed. I believe that when someone is in the grips of depression, their spirit is very low, which means their life force is diminished. In Chinese medicine, Chi energy is our life force and the vital energy that circulates through the body at all times. When someone has a Chi deficiency, it is thought of as an imbalance, and can be linked to the spleen. What is usually prescribed is rest, herbs, and eating certain foods to replenish the Chi so it can circulate better and make the patient feel healthy again. But, if we don't add to that, feeding our soul, which replenishes our spirit, we are only treating part of the problem, and our

Chi, or life force will begin to weaken again.

So, how do we feed our spirit properly? What kind of diet can we maintain to make sure that it is being nurtured so we can feel vital and enthusiastic about our life? In Christianity, the Bible identifies humanity's three basic elements as "spirit, soul and body," and that the human spirit is the "real person, the very core of a person's being, the essential seat of their existence." That's the authentic self I talk about. If we are not living our life as who we truly are, our spirit will feel suffocated, and gradually our life force, the Chi that's supposed to be circulating throughout our body at all times is being sucked right out of us. As Dorothy Day's quote above says, "Food for the body is not enough. There must be food for the soul."

How are you tending to your spirit so it can feed your soul properly? Do you wake up each morning feeling energized and excited? Okay, not every day do we wake up feeling invigorated or enthusiastic about starting our day, but the reason for that, most often, is that there is an underlying cause, and we don't know what it is. Many people go through life feeling very unenthusiastic, even listless or apathetic. They basically amble along, going through the motions of being alive, but barely are. Depression is one of the most common mental disorders in the United States, and suicide rates have increased by 25% in the last two decades. I talked about the Opioid crisis, which is epidemic. Millions of people are walking around anything but invigorated or excited about life, and instead choosing to numb out in some way, which is anathema for the spirit.

An image for that is a homicidal one, meaning you are literally killing your life force, as if by asphyxiation. You may not know this when you choose to numb yourself, or escape from your pain or unhappiness by avoiding it, but you are actually starving your spirit by depriving it of the very oxygen it needs. The spirit wants nothing more than to be lifted naturally. It wants to "trip the light fantastic," which I spoke about in Chapter 14 - The Cosmic Dance. Yes, the spirit wants to move nimbly in our body, full of energy and vitality. Milton was referring to dancing in his quote, and life, as I said, is a cosmic dance. But we cannot move through it if we don't, as Thich Nhat Hahn says in part of his quote, "touch the miracle of being alive." Yes, "many people are alive," as the full quote goes, but if you aren't aware or conscious of what a true miracle it is to be alive, then your spirit will suffer because you are not allowing it to touch you and lift you higher.

This brings us back to Mindfulness, and how we must be present so that we can know when our spirit needs tending to and can properly give it what it requires. The human spirit is the "very core of our being" and the "essential seat of our existence." If we don't feed and nurture our spirit properly, it will invariably suffer. In Jewish mysticism, there is something called "Chokhmah." This is the all-encompassing "Supernal Wisdom" that vitalizes all of creation. We, too, need to connect to our own supernal wisdom, which means a type of wisdom that is defined as coming from "on high" or the "heavens." I spoke about this in Chapter 5 - Divine Thought Illumination. I said that I view divine illumination as "thinking that is guided by light."

And this is what our human spirit needs. It needs us to hold thoughts in our mind that are "guided by light." And, by doing so, we are connecting to our supernal wisdom, a type of wisdom that is "godly" or "heavenly." This is walking the mystical path, and a path, I believe, intended for the human spirit. What other path do we feel is meant for us other than to be "in union with reality?" This is the reality of oneness, also called unity consciousness. As I said, this means we are in union, first and foremost, with ourselves, so that we can be in union with all that exists. This is what our spirit hungers for.

But, it takes a genuine effort on our part to provide this path for our spirit, and our spirit deserves nothing less than a path of higher wisdom to feed it each day. This means we practice Mindfulness, present moment awareness, and keep our thoughts illumined so that we can be in a state of heightened awareness, and our consciousness can stay on an upwardly mobile trajectory. If we abandon our commitment to keep our authentic-self most vital, then we are abandoning our spirit, our soul and ultimately, Anima Mundi, the soul of the world.

As Stephen Hawking said, "We are all different. There is no such thing as a standard or run-of-the-mill human being, but we share the same human spirit." This means that each of our spirit is part of Anima Mundi, the soul of the world, and if our spirit is low, or suffering, the soul of the world is suffering. It seems, at times, that the soul of the world is, indeed, suffering. We may be individual beings, but if you subscribe to the belief that we are not separate, but joined as one organism, which is oneness, or unity consciousness, then our spirit is connected to all that exists. If that doesn't invigorate us, I don't know what will. The mystical experiences of Evelyn Underhill and Jane Goodall tell us that this oneness is real, and that realness is realized when we are in union with reality. And, that reality lets us know that we are not separate, but, in fact, connected to everything.

This realization can come to us when we are in a heightened state of awareness, but unfortunately, we are not in this state as much as we can be, and it deprives our spirit when we're not. Our spirit not only deserves to be nurtured and loved, but also to feel exalted, and that's when we can feel the type of joy and bliss that gets our neurotransmitters really fired up. As I've said, that's about as naturally high as you can get. That's when you can feel sensations of ecstasy that many mystics have described. But remember, those types of sensations are not just meant only for the mystic. The mystical experience awaits each of us, if we are open to it. But, you cannot even come close to it if you are ignoring your spirit. He who ignores, or does not feed his spirit, may never taste the exquisite flavor of the mystical, let alone the "after-flavor of it" as Underhill described, and that is like being robbed of the most delectable foods and flavors we can taste.

When we are good to ourselves, and value who we are, we are, in essence, taking care of our spirit, which makes it more likely for us to be in union with reality so that we can feel happiness and experience bouts of joyous exaltation. When we eat well, and exercise, we are taking care of our body to keep healthy and fit, but we don't usually think of ways to take care of our spirit with the same kind of attentiveness. If we viewed our spirit as something that needs just as much care, if not more because it is "the very core of our being, the essential seat of our existence" then we would make sure that when we wake up each day, and before we do anything else, we take our spiritual pulse and connect to the core of our being. This will always help gauge the Chi energy of your spirit, your vital life force to know whether it needs nurturing and balancing. And if it does, you will take the time to do it.

Remember, your spirit must be fed, and that could mean anything from meditating, practicing yoga, sitting in contemplation, taking a walk on the beach, gardening, playing with an animal, making love, painting, cooking, serving someone in need, or moving to music (like I suggested in the cosmic dance exercise I gave you in Chapter 14). Get in the habit of doing these types of things and your spirit will thank you by how invigorated and high-spirited you feel.

Here is something you can do to connect to the core of your being daily.

1. When you open your eyes in the morning, take a few moments to connect to your breath.
2. Put your hands on your heart, and feel your chest rising and falling with each breath.
3. Acknowledge your spirit as your life force.
4. Imagine it as a powerful source of energy moving throughout your entire body.
5. Say silently, "I care for my spirit."
6. Say silently, "I do all that I can to keep my spirit healthy and vital."
7. Say silently, "I am a spiritual being."

We must take the time to go within ourselves at some point in our day, and the best way to start each day is by connecting to our spirit. Whether you meditate or not, find at least ten minutes each day to be quiet with yourself, and connect to your core, the seat of your existence. Listen to your spirit and hear what it has to say. It will tell you what it needs, and the kindest thing you can do is give it what it desires so it can thrive.

My spirit
Breathes life into me
Each and every day
I acknowledge it
I listen to it
And I allow for it
To guide me
In all that I do

MINDFULNESS & MYSTICISM

CHAPTER 17

ADDICTION AND MYSTICISM

I have absolutely no pleasure in the stimulants in which I sometimes madly indulge.

It has not been in the pursuit of pleasure that I have periled life and reputation and reason.

It has been the desperate attempt to escape from torturing memories, from a sense of insupportable loneliness, and a dread of some strange impending doom.

— EDGAR ALLAN POE

Every form of addiction is bad, no matter whether the narcotic be alcohol or morphine or idealism.

— CARL JUNG

That which does not kill us makes us stronger.

— FREDRICH NIETZSCHE

The American Society of Addiction Medicine (ASAM) has both a short and long definition of addiction. This is part of the short one: "Addiction is a primary, chronic disease of brain reward, motivation, memory and related circuitry. Dysfunction in these circuits leads to characteristic, biological, psychological, social and spiritual manifestations. This is reflected in an individual pathologically pursuing reward and/or relief by substance use and other behaviors."

What stands out about this definition for me is "chronic disease of brain reward," which touches on some of what I have discussed about our brain, and brain chemistry. I am not a neuroscientist, nor a doctor, and do not profess to know about the imbalances of brain chemistry. What I have chosen to focus on in this book are the extraordinary aspects of who we are, and that includes the brains remarkable ability to not only produce neurotransmitters that can make us feel as good, or as high as any drug can, but can also heal itself through neuroplasticity, which is the brain's ability to "reorganize itself by forming new neural connections throughout life."

The one word that usually accompanies the definition of addiction is "disease," but if scientists are realizing the brain's ability to heal itself, wouldn't that mean that the "dysfunction" in the brain's circuits, which the American Society of Addiction Medicine describes in its definition of addiction, can be repaired?

When explanations like "disease" or "dysfunction" are used for addiction, which is a condition that plagues millions of people, it makes sense to me that over time, like anything else we research and learn more about, we will find that it doesn't stop there, meaning that it's not just about the disease or the dysfunction that can tell us everything we need to know about addiction, but something much more than that, and new discoveries are being made at a rapid speed.

The idea that mental disorders are caused by a chemical imbalance in the brain was first proposed by scientists in the late 1950s, and research at the time had focused on the role that chemicals in the brain play in depression and anxiety. But now with scientific discoveries in the area of neuroplasticity, it's showing that chemical imbalances can be changed and repaired. I prefer thinking of addiction as something that can be healed and repaired, rather than only speak of it as a "disease" or "dysfunction," which gets stuck in a definition that seems limited and outdated.

You're going to have many people like myself weigh in on addiction other than just doctors, and, as we know, there are many theories about addiction, its causes, and its treatments. I happen to lean more towards what author, and creator of MBSR, Mindfulness Based Stress Reduction, Jon Kabat-Zinn says, "All the suffering, stress and addiction comes from not realizing you already are what you are looking for." Does that mean addicts don't have chemical imbalances, or dysfunction in their brain circuits, or a "chronic disease of brain reward, motivation, memory and related circuitry?" Perhaps. We probably shouldn't rule anything out, but staying with, or relying on explanations like "disease" or "dysfunction" as the only reasons for addiction, is, as I said, limited and outdated, and that is anything but mystical, which is exactly where I want to go with this.

Mysticism also can stay stuck in definitions and explanations that are limited and outdated, and for the most part, it's not a word people fold into everyday conversation. That's why I want to dispel the mystery around it. I use mysticism in relation to spirituality, meaning all that concerns the spirit and the soul. We don't usually talk about the spirit and the soul, but we should. As a matter of fact, I believe if we did talk about what breathes life into our bodies (our spirit) and gives depth to our being (our soul), we probably would be much better at addressing what truly ails us, and causes us so much pain and suffering. If you go by Edgar Allan Poe's quote above, it was not his "pursuit of pleasure" that he "periled life and reputation" it was his "desperate attempt to escape from torturing memories, a sense of insupportable loneliness, and a dread of some strange impending doom."

I would venture to say that if you asked many addicts whether they have ever felt this way, you would probably get a resounding "yes!" We are human, and we are going to suffer and feel lonely, and have some very unpleasant, even "torturing memories," as Poe said. And how about a feeling of "some strange impending doom?" What Edgar Allan Poe describes is universal. It's as if he were speaking about a day in the life of millions of people, the human condition, and the struggles we face being alive.

But it is what we do with our suffering that will make all the difference in the world, as to whether we reach out for a substance to numb it or not. Does someone with addiction in their family stand a greater chance going the drug or alcohol route when difficulty arises versus someone who has no addiction in their family history? Again, perhaps. If that's the case, how do you explain family members who share similar DNA, or were exposed to the same trauma, and one becomes an addict, and the other(s) don't? Is that nature versus nurture, genetic inheritance, or environmental factors?

I understand there are many factors to consider when it comes to addiction, or what makes someone an addict, and the controversy continues over whether addiction is truly a disease or not. One theory is that it is not a disease, but a choice, which immediately brings to mind the following: why would anyone choose to be an addict? It could be for a variety of reasons, but I'd like to focus on what lies beneath our choices, especially if they are destructive and harmful to us, which addiction is, and it brings me right back to mysticism.

Mysticism, as it's been defined, especially by those who have had mystical experiences, is being "in union" or "at one with" something greater than the self. It has been described as "in union with reality" as Underhill said, and that reality, as I've discussed, is a non-separateness from God, unity consciousness, source, oneness, or whatever you want to call something that is divine, holy and sacred. Whether it's religious, or philosophical, mysticism lets us know that there is something more than who we are in this body, and if you believe it, and allow for it to show you this non-separateness, you will feel something that can best be described as holy, sacred, and divine, and when you do, suffering can disappear completely.

An addict doesn't ask to be united with something holy, sacred, or divine when they reach for a drug or alcohol. Instead, they want to avoid and numb their pain. I don't know what an addict says to themselves privately, and maybe there have been those who spoke to God, or source, or a power greater than themselves, and asked to be "at one" with something that could take away, or end their suffering, even if it was for as long as their high lasted.

It's interesting that in Alcoholics Anonymous (AA), which has been called a "spiritual movement" and a "faith cure for alcoholism," its members are asked to believe in a higher being as an integral part of their recovery. Many of them realize that they have lived without God, and now, through the program, learn how to live believing in God, or whatever their own concept of God is. Whatever their belief is, they are asked to "obey a Higher Power as they understand it" and surrender to this power for guidance to keep them clean and sober.

Wouldn't it be great if we learned how to connect to our own spirit, as I spoke about in Chapter 16 - The Human Spirit, and began each day taking our spiritual pulse to know how we're doing deep in our soul? No matter what difficulty we are having, or sadness we're feeling, our spirit is not going to tell us to numb ourselves, because, as I said, that is anathema for the spirit. It does not want to be numbed or silenced, but instead listened to very carefully so that it may guide us to be in union with reality, and not separate from a "Higher Power greater than ourselves." I believe that most addicts are in so much emotional pain, and tormented by their "torturing memories" as Edgar Allan Poe said, and feel such "insupportable loneliness" and "a dread of some impending doom" that there is no interest in connecting with their spirit because when you're desperate, the only thing you want to do is deprive yourself of feeling anything. This means anesthetizing your pain to deaden what torments you. You completely bypass connecting to spirit, and yet, when you have admitted to yourself that you are an addict, and choose to seek help, that is what you are asked to do in AA: "obey a Higher Power greater than yourself" to guide you.

So now the addict, if they haven't killed themselves, and instead, want to be helped, healed, or saved, realizes they must believe in a "Higher Power greater than themselves." What they might not know is that this "Higher Power greater than themselves" was there all along. Perhaps Saint Augustine was correct when he said, "You will light my lamp, Lord. You hear nothing true from me which you have not first told me," and the only way one can experience divine illumination is through "supernatural assistance." For some, they believe their lamp is lit from within, and do not need God's assistance; and for others, they need the help desperately, as many addicts do. How tragic to wait until one is upon death's door to ask for help, or "God's assistance." Sadly, for many addicts, neither God, nor any other force, could save them because the drug, or alcohol won out. Their spirit, their life force, or the "very core of a person's being, the essential seat of their existence" no longer breathes in their body.

What is it that we remember about a loved one when they are no longer here? Do we mourn their body? No, we mourn their spirit, the core of their being, their very existence. We think of their vital life force, and how it moved through them and made them smile, and laugh, and cry. That is what we miss, their inimitable spirit that was solely their own, and that's what we loved so much about them.

The spirit, for the addict, is extremely important to pay attention to. There is a famous exchange between the great psychiatrist Dr. Carl Jung, who helped influence the spiritual roots of Alcoholics Anonymous, and an American alcoholic named Rowland Hazard. He was sent to Zurich, Switzerland to Dr. Jung's clinic. Jung told Rowland that since they were unable to bring about a psychic change in him, he would be discharged. Rowland, completely startled asked: "Is there no hope for me, then?" Dr. Jung's answer was, "No, there is none except for some people with your problem have recovered if they have had a transforming experience of the spirit." (Wilson/Jung Letters, 1987).

Jung believed that the addict had to experience a "genuine conversion," which was a "spiritual experience stronger than the craving of alcohol." And this is what a mystical experience can do. It can transcend a craving, and there are many people who have stopped their addictive patterns and behaviors cold turkey, and never looked back. Keep in mind that a mystical experience can be something like what we would refer to as an "aha moment" or an epiphany. In that moment, it's as if a light goes off in your head, and a "conversion" happens right then and there. You are "transformed."

Bill Wilson, the co-founder of AA, and an alcoholic, was said to have had such a conversion.

"I sunk into the most unbearable depression that I had ever known. I suppose that momentarily, at least, that the last vestige of my prideful obstinacy was crushed out. I was just a child, crying alone, very alone in the dark. For the extremity of this agony, I could find no words. And then I remember crying out, 'If there be a God, will he show himself?'"

It was this mystical experience that became known in AA as "Bill's white light transformation."

"The room instantly lit up, lit up in a blinding glare

of white, white light. I was seized by an ecstasy, such as I had never known. It seemed to me, that I then stood on a mountain top, where a great, clean wind was blowing. I thought to myself, but this is not air, this is spirit. This is the God of the preachers. How long I remained in this state, I just cannot say. And, again, I have no words to describe what it was like. At length, however, I found myself on the bed, but now I was in a new world. A world in which everything was right, despite the wrongs of the world I had been living in. I felt myself filled with a consciousness of the presence of spirit; of God. A great peace stole over me. And there I laid and reveled in this new and loving consciousness" (Bill and Lois tell their story – YouTube).

Wilson never drank again. Jung told Wilson that his craving for alcohol "was the equivalent, on a low level, of the spiritual thirst of our being for wholeness; the union with God." This transformational experience, I believe, is realizing, as William Blake says in his quote, "I am in you and you in me, mutual in divine love." And that is what mysticism reveals to us. That "divine love" is in us always. We just need to believe it. There is no drug, or excessive use of alcohol, that can give us the supernal wisdom, a deeper, more spiritual understanding of life. This is knowing that we are whole, and not separate from God, or whatever the divine means to us. Why must we choose, instead, to suffer? As Buddha said, "Pain is inevitable, suffering is optional."

The mystical experience awaits each of us. If you think you might be an addict, or know for sure that you are, do you want to continue being one? Or, if you believe that addiction is a disease, and you have this disease, ask yourself the following: "Do I wish to be healed from my disease?"

Disease means, "lack of ease." And that means there is discomfort, or lack of ease, within you, and you must get to the bottom of it to be cured of it. Drugs or alcohol may ease discomfort or tension, but only for a while, which is why there is a need to keep having more. The only way to heal oneself from the discomfort, or lack of ease that causes disruption or imbalance in the body, is to heal the whole person, mind, body, and spirit. This is what the addict needs more than anything, to have a complete healing, especially of the spirit. Ignoring the spirit, as I said, is a type of asphyxiation, and for the addict, it is especially dangerous because if they lose connection to the most vital part of their life force, their spirit, death is often inevitable. The number one most important question an addict should ask themselves is, "Do I want to live or die?"

The following are additional questions to ask yourself
if addiction is something with which you are grappling:

1. "Am I an addict?"
2. If you answered "yes," ask yourself, "What am I
   addicted to?"
3. "Why am I addicted to (whatever you are addicted
   to)?"
4. "Do I want to stay addicted to (whatever you are
   addicted to)?"
5. "Do I have to stay addicted to (whatever you are
   addicted to)?"
6. "What is it about the high I like?"
7. "What is it about the high I need?"
8. "Who am I when I am high?"
9. "Who am I when I am not high?"
10. "What is missing in my life that makes me want
    to get high?"
11. "Is there something troubling my soul?"
12. "What if there was a divine energy that could fill
    my soul each day?"
13. "What if this divine energy was within me?"
14. "What if this divine energy could make me high
    naturally?"
15. "Do I want to experience this divine energy?"
16. "Am I ready to let this divine energy heal me?"
17. Say to yourself, "I am ready to be filled with
    divine love."

An addict doesn't think of themselves as a healer, and yet, they have the ability to heal if they took their spiritual pulse and listened to their spirit. Think of the spirit as the voice of the soul. It can speak to us at any given moment of our day and tell us what our soul yearns for. We may think it's a substance, but that substance is only masking something much deeper that the soul is yearning for. It is yearning for "divine love." Yes, that is what the soul wants, and that is all that it needs. But, we will poison our body with drugs, or excessive use of alcohol thinking we are satisfying something that we need. It can make you desperate, and "peril" your "life and reputation," as Edgar Allan Poe described it.

I can tell you that there is no greater high than the mystical experience, and you might think, "How do I experience it?" You begin by listening to your spirit, and asking it to guide you. And, if you're in recovery and believe that a "Higher Power greater than you" is helping you stay on the path of sobriety, ask it to guide you towards the mystical. But here's what I want you to know. You are choosing this. You are choosing to be sober, and now you are choosing to listen to your spirit. You can continue to make wise choices for yourself every single moment of your life.

And know this: "Between stimulus and response there is a space. In that space is our power to choose our response. In our response lies our growth and our freedom" (Victor E. Frankl).

I crave

Nothing more than

Freedom from addiction

I am in union

With the divine

It breathes life

Into my spirit

MINDFULNESS & MYSTICISM

CHAPTER 18

ASCENDING THROUGH CONTEMPLATION

Contemplation is life itself, fully awake,
fully active, and fully aware that it is alive.
It is a spiritual wonder.
It is spontaneous awe at the
sacredness of life, of being.
It is gratitude for life, for
awareness, and for being.
It is a vivid realization of the fact that
life and being in us proceed from an invisible,
transcendent, and infinitely abundant source.

— THOMAS MERTON

If each man contemplated his existence, and pondered deeply the meaning of life, he would come to know that there is something greater than himself. That realization as monk, theologian, and mystic Thomas Merton says in his quote above is this: "That life and being in us proceed from an invisible, transcendent, and infinitely abundant source."

And, that source, as I've talked about, is different for each of us. But to know it, if one chooses to know what lies beyond what I call the first layer of truth, or the surface of life, is "infinitely abundant," as Merton says. But, we most often don't go towards this abundant source because we choose not to be still, or as it says in the Old Testament (Psalm 46:10): "Be still and know that I am God." This is a religious interpretation of stillness so we may be in union with something divine, holy, or sacred. Contemplation, a "spiritual wonder," as Merton describes it unites us with it. The Hebrew definition of "be still and know" is to "stop striving, to let go, surrender" so that we can take comfort in letting go and resting there so that God, or a Divine source, can provide "help, strength and safety." But how can we do this if we don't make time for being in "union with reality," that greater connection to the "invisible," the "transcendent," and "infinitely abundant source" to which Merton refers?

If we don't stop, even occasionally, we are disconnected and removed from a source greater than us from where we can sit and know. And this knowing can only be known in the quietude and stillness of non-doing. We cannot avoid a stillness that lets us glimpse into divine love, for which our soul longs. If we keep hoping we can realize it outside of ourselves, and endlessly search for it, we will remain terribly disappointed when it eludes us. And, divine love will always elude us if we are constantly looking for it externally, or in another. This does not mean we can't love someone deeply, or that such a thing can't be described as divine. We can, but our love for them can diminish with time because we expect love to keep taking us to greater heights, which is the high and euphoria I've spoken about. Love can take us to great heights, but we will be dropped from its elevation if we don't meet it with a greater love we must realize on our own. And this love is "transcendent" and "abundant," which we must bring to every moment of our life to stay in a heightened state of awareness and continue to raise our consciousness.

Contemplation helps us raise our consciousness by spending time looking at what consciousness means. It is only by our own deep examining, and looking at the great themes of life very closely, that we can we know more about ourselves, the universe, and our role in it. And, this is what contemplation does. It lets us ponder who we are, and why we are here. We can only experience this if we sit patiently so we may receive answers that can help us know. We cannot rush in our sitting, but sit quietly, as if waiting to be called, summoned by the "transcendent," the mystical, even if it is "invisible." And we must learn how to accept what we cannot see, but trust in our heart that it is real. The mystical is not always visible to the eye. It does not always have a shape, or a sound, or a smell. It can transcend the senses and go beyond the physical, but it is there like a spirit we may not see in human form, yet can feel. It is that "awe-inspiring" feeling, which many have described in their mystical experiences, and can be hard to put into words, but in our stillness with it, we know, yes, we know that there is something greater than us, and it moves us so deeply that divine love is the perfect description for it.

Sitting quietly, deep in contemplation, helps us cultivate a familiarity with where our soul can rest and feel safe. We cannot know this feeling when we are hiding from it, or running from it, or staying so busy that we don't go within ourselves long enough to connect to our soul's inner sanctum. We must ask ourselves why do we run from this? What is it that keeps us from ourselves, from receiving a greater knowing of who we are? Is it frightening to know the authentic-self? To experience the self-surrender that I spoke about in Chapter 7 - Self-Surrender, and free fall into who we really are, lifting the veils of all that is false? Does this frighten you, or are you ready to sit quietly and venture deeper into yourself?

Contemplation is sacred, like the mystical experience, and if you desire it, all it asks of you is to be willing to sit so that you may know. You may come to know that God is within you by what God tells you. But you must listen, and listen well. Whether it's God, or a Divine presence that sits with you, know that it wants you to be aware of the "sacredness of life," and this is what present moment awareness does for us. It not only says, "be still and know," but it also says, again and again, "this moment right now is sacred, holy, and divine," and God, or source, is always present in it. Why would we rush out of it? Why wouldn't we sit in deep contemplation with what is most sacred, holy, and divine? Don't we realize that we are always running from it? Can you imagine? We are running away from what is most sacred and divine, and then wonder why our soul feels empty, and love continues to disappoint or elude us, and we run more, hoping that we can catch what keeps slipping from our grasp, oneness; the fundamental union with reality.

We can enter this exquisite, mystical state of oneness, also called Henosis, which Greek philosopher Plotinus believed we could achieve in contemplation. It is in stillness that the mystical can penetrate us. Are you still wondering what it is, or if you will ever experience it? Maybe you have, and long to experience it again, and aren't quite sure how you experienced it in the first place. Well, I can assure you that you weren't hiding, or running, or afraid. You were open, and you were present, and you were accepting of who you were in the moment. Can you recall having a moment such as this? Can you see that you might have had a mystical experience and maybe didn't know it? I had mystical experiences that began as a young girl and didn't know it. I had no words for it. I felt waves of ecstasy, and a deep connection to everything around me, but did not know that these were mystical experiences, and they were, even if they were fleeting.

We are smart, intelligent human beings, are we not? And yet, we avoid the very bliss, the ecstasy of knowing what this life is. When we glimpse it, it's as Evelyn Underhill says: "When one does catch it, it is so real that to look upon it as wrong would be an unthinkable absurdity." It does seem absurd to not let ourselves "catch it," and we can, if we do things like stop our busyness, and sit in contemplation.

Let me guide you in sitting, and ease you into contemplation so that it becomes a natural state of consciousness for you.

1. Find a quiet place to sit.
2. Let your mind rest in non-doing.
3. Open your mind to receive wisdom by telling yourself you are open to knowing it.
4. If your mind is active, engage it in a question.
5. For example, ask yourself the following:

   a. "Who am I?"

   b. "What is this life?"

   c. What is my purpose in this life?"

   d. "What is the meaning of existence?"

   e. "What is my soul?"

   f. "What is my spirit?"

   g. "Where does my spirit go when it leaves this body?"

6. Spend time allowing yourself to be with what you ask, and call forward God, source, or whatever the Divine means for you.

7. Say that you are ready to "know."

8. Be with whatever you are hearing or feeling.

9. Allow yourself to go deeper into reflective thinking.

10. Let your introspection take you where it will.

11. Surrender to a state of mystical awareness.

12. Let yourself free fall into a connection between your soul and the divine.

Contemplation can be very mystical and has been described as the soul journeying toward the union with God, or divine union. I ask again: Is this what we secretly long for? To be in union with something that speaks directly to our soul and tells us the spiritual truth we wish to know? Priest, and theologian Saint Thomas Aquinas defined contemplation as a "simple gaze on truth." If we wish to know this truth, we must sit, and we must also be willing to wait with patience. We cannot hurry these

messages to be told to us, any more than we can insist on
having a mystical experience. We will hear them when
we are ready to. The messages we receive in deep contemplation are considered gifts, and whether they are direct
messages from God, or a Divine, holy source we choose
to name, we mustn't make light of them, or take them
for granted. Sitting in contemplation is, in itself, having
regard for the silence. By holding space in contemplation
for something deep or profound to be known, we stand a
greater chance of knowing it. Sit, and again, tell yourself
you are ready to know.

Contemplation mustn't be confused with meditation, which is another form of sitting, but is intended to
quiet the mind so it does not wander aimlessly. Both are
meant for spiritual growth, and can help bring us closer
to knowing who we are. The difference between them has
been described as follows: meditation is something we do,
and contemplation is where we can receive. Making time
for both, or either, is a gift to ourselves. But it is in stillness that we make room to know. Find time in your day
to be still so that you may know more of who you are, and
in your knowing, be in union with reality.

I sit

And I know

I sit again

So that I may know more

It is in stillness

I hear the voice of

Divine love

I am in union

With it

MINDFULNESS & MYSTICISM

CHAPTER 19

DARK NIGHT OF THE SOUL

Being human is a complicated gig. So, give that ol' dark night of the soul a hug. Howl the eternal yes!

— FREDRICH NIETZSCHE

The dark night of the soul comes just before revelation.

— JOSEPH CAMPBELL

Won't You guide me through the dark night of the soul that I may understand your way…Let me purify my thoughts and words and deeds that I may be a vehicle for Thee — Give me my rapture today.

— VAN MORRISON

When I speak of the mystical experience, I describe it with words such as ecstasy, euphoria, and bliss, and when we read about those who have had the mystical experiences I've shared thus far like Evelyn Underhill, Jane Goodall, and AA co-founder, Bill Wilson we can glean that they all experienced a type of rapture, or spiritual ecstasy that seemed life changing.

It can be an experience of "transformation" where something profound can be realized, and you are changed somehow, even if you don't know exactly in what way at the time. Bill Wilson explained it as follows: "I was in a new world. A world in which everything was right, despite the wrongs of the world I had been living in. I felt myself filled with a consciousness of the presence of spirit; of God. A great peace stole over me. And there I laid and reveled in this new and loving consciousness." His mystical experience, or what has been referred to as "Bill's white light transformation," changed his life forever, and he never drank again.

Mystical experiences can be had in a variety of ways. As a young girl, I had bouts of unexpected ecstasy, which I've mentioned, and feel that was my introduction into the mystical experience. I also remember having lucid dreams, as well as nightmares that were teeming with symbolism, and I considered those mystical, too. But it wasn't until years later when I had episodes of what could be called an "existential crisis," that I can now say were some of the most profound mystical experiences I had.

It was when my soul felt frightened and desolate that I found myself praying to an unseen presence, and I know deep in my heart that I was listened to, even though that presence was invisible.

Yes, there are many different ways to have a mystical experience, and not all of them are euphoric or blissful, which brings us to the dark night of the soul. Even when one is experiencing "spiritual desolation," as it has been described, something mystical can happen. If we don't resist or fight it, it will lead us to where we need to go and tell us what we need to know.

If we think of the dark night of the soul as something each of us will experience at some point in our lives, we might agree with Flannery O'Conner when she says, "Right now the whole world seems to be going through a dark night of the soul" and maybe it is. I spoke about Anima Mundi, the soul of the world, and if we view this life as a stream of consciousness always evolving, there have been dark periods throughout history that seemed as if they would never end. Humanity and spiritual evolution were in question. Great transformation can come from the darkness, but if we haven't learned from it, then darkness remains deep in our soul, and in the soul of the world.

A dark night of the soul can be one of the most powerful mystical experiences you can go through, and if you surrender, or free fall, as I've called it, you can have an awakening like no other. And that's what the dark night of the soul is meant to do, to awaken you from the slumber of your unconsciousness. I spoke about this in Chapter 3 - Awaken Now, when I said, "You may be alive, but that does not mean you are awake, consciously."

The awakening can happen when you are gripped by the dark night, and feel as if your heart is being ripped from your chest. You may find yourself begging God, or a Divine source to give you soothing comfort. It is called the "dark night of the soul" because it is through the darkness that your soul must find the light again.

In Roman Catholic spirituality, dark night of the soul means that one is having a spiritual crisis, also referred to as a spiritual "emergency." That can also mean an existential crisis, which I mentioned I had experienced, and that is when you question whether your life has "meaning, purpose, or value." This question can be answered, not when one is in crisis, but instead, when one is taking what I have called your spiritual pulse. Checking in with ourselves to find out how we are doing is something I recommend daily. Again, I can't emphasize enough how important it is to tend to our spirit, our vital life force, before it is so depleted or starved that a crisis is inevitable, and the soul finds itself stumbling in the dark, fearing no way out.

The dark night of the soul can cause someone to plunge deeper into darkness and despair, and for many, it can last a lot longer than a night. It is said that Spanish Mystic and poet, St. John of the Cross suffered his own spiritual crisis that lasted for 45 years, but he ultimately recovered. It is hard to imagine this type of unbearable darkness lasting for such a long period of time, but in the case of St. John of the Cross, he poured his journey of darkness into epic writing, like his poems, "The Dark Night" and "Ascent of Mount Carmel," which is about the pursuit of a mystical union with Christ. St. John writes of the journey of the dark night as the soul's yearning to have a "mystical union with God," which it has not realized because God is "unknowable" and the cause of suffering. He writes of his union with God in his poem, and in stanza four says this:

> "This guided me
> More surely than the light of noon
> To where he was awaiting me
> -him I knew so well-
> There in a place where no one appeared."

You get a sense of his "union" when he writes in stanza 5:

> "O guiding night!
> O night more lovely than the dawn!
> O night that has united
> The lover with his beloved,
> Transforming the beloved in her lover."

And this is what being "in union with reality" means. There is no separation between us and God, or a Divine source that is personal for us. When we are disconnected from our own spirit, God, or whatever Divine essence we hold deep in our heart, suffering begins, and it can grow to such deep despair, one finds one's self reaching for drugs or alcohol to ameliorate the pain and suffering. What comes next is the dark night, and it can be the blackest of darkness there is.

When gripped by darkness, it's not so easy to feel that it is a night, as St. John says, "more lovely than the dawn!" For many people who are taken over by darkness, there is no dawn in sight, which is why suicide is often the answer for those who believe there is no way out from the bleak darkness they feel in their soul. This reminds me of French philosopher Jean Paul Sartre's play, "No Exit." It's an existential play about three characters who find themselves in a mysterious room that turns out to be hell. They are put there as a punishment to ponder their crimes. And that's what the dark night of the soul can feel like, hell. But it is a hell in which we put ourselves in, and it is a hell from which we can remove ourselves. There is an exit from the dark night, but we must reach deep into our soul, and ask our spirit to help guide us from the darkness and it will.

Our spirit is our vital life force, as I said. It is our beacon on the life journey where darkness is inevitable.

If we do not connect to it, we will feel darkness in our soul. Do not wait until your sadness, depression or despair is so great that you feel hopeless. Awaken each day and be present and mindfully aware of the "very core of your being." Say hello to your spirit, as if you are greeting God, source, or whatever you want to call Divine Presence, and be a gracious host. Invite holiness into your home, your sacred temple of self. Are you not worthy of such a visit?

You needn't be religious to invite holiness into your soul, but you do need to be open to being in "union with reality" so that the mystical can come to you, and it will, as I've said. It may not come to you in an immediate, life-altering way. The mystical experience can come in many different ways. And, it can happen unexpectedly. If you are open, and not disconnected from your spirit, you are ready for a mystical awakening. It can be subtle, or it can be bold. Your job is not to let yourself slip into the dark night. Yes, you can have a mystical experience as you are drowning in darkness, but do you want that? Must you wait for your soul to be saved while in the grips of darkness that feels like hell?

Do not do this to yourself. Take your spiritual pulse daily. Know what is stirring in your heart. And ask to be embraced in Divine Love. This is what our soul wants. Give it to yours, and your spirit will purr like a kitten.

The night is dark
And my soul feels blind
But I know that light
Is here in the darkness
Come to me
Light of holy knowing
And embrace me in
Divine love

MINDFULNESS & MYSTICISM

CHAPTER 20

VISITS OF ECSTASY

You do not need to leave your room. Remain sitting at your table and listen. Do not even listen, simply wait, be quiet still and solitary. The world will freely offer itself to you to be unmasked, it has no choice, it will roll in ecstasy at your feet.

— FRANZ KAFKA

The highest ecstasy is the attention at its fullest.

— SIMONE WEIL

There is a fine line between pain and ecstasy. For poet Charles Baudelaire, he experienced it this way: "As a small child, I felt in my heart two contradictory feelings, the horror of life and the ecstasy of life."

Life certainly can be horrific, but it can also envelop us in such a deep feeling of ecstasy, it seems as if there is no hell in sight, only heaven on earth. I mentioned that Mindfulness helps keep hell at bay by keeping us so present, we value each moment as a gift to be alive. We are not only aware of life's difficulties and "horrors," but also acknowledge the impermanence of this life; so therefore, we make a concerted effort to seek ecstasy over horror while we are here.

And this brings us back to "choices," which I spoke about in Chapter 17 - Addiction and Mysticism. As Buddha said, "Pain is inevitable, suffering is optional." It's not as if we choose either pain or suffering, but the pain we will experience in this life is inevitable, so we must choose to approach suffering in a way that does not keep us a hostage to it.

We must stay connected to our spirit, so that it may give us the energy we need to keep going especially when times are rough, and we view our glass as filled with more horror than ecstasy. The steps I have walked you through so far are meant for you to stay present, and understand you are not separate from God, or a Divine presence, but "at one" with all that exists. As Carl Sagan says in this quote, "Understanding is a kind of ecstasy."

The deeper your understanding is about you, this life, and your purpose here, the more likely you are to experience visits of ecstasy, as this chapter is called. And these visits which are like a breeze coming through a window, or a waft of a delicious aroma, or flowers delivered on a special occasion, or someone saying "I love you" when your heart needs it the most, are moments of ecstasy that come unexpectedly. Suddenly you feel as if all of the molecules and atoms in the universe, and in your entire being are breathing as one organism. And, even if that feeling lasts less than a minute, you know that as difficult, or even horrible, as life can be, ecstasy is on the other side of it. It will come to you again and again because ecstasy, like God, or Divine presence, is always there.

Visits of ecstasy are like mini mystical experiences. You might be very surprised that you've had them, but never acknowledged them as anything other than having a really nice moment. You might have said, "That was so great!" or "That felt so good!" Or when something fills us with great joy, we say, "I am so happy!" or even, "This is the best moment of my life!" Happiness is a form of ecstasy, and what fills us with happiness is food for our soul. If we let ourselves free fall into our happiness, and drop into the abundance it brings us, we can take that feeling and let it grow and heighten. The next thing you know you feel giddy with happiness, even ecstatic.

Like the mystical experience, we can't force a feeling

of ecstasy. But, if we avail ourselves to life in a way that isn't begrudging, or resent the difficulties or horrors it has shown us, you needn't do much for ecstasy to "roll at your feet," as Kafka says. You just have to believe that in spite of your disappointments, hurts and sorrows, you deserve to feel a type of joy and delight that can enrapture you. This ecstasy I'm talking about isn't a synthetic drug like MDMA, which can alter mood and perception, and increase a feeling of energy and pleasure. Millions of people take this drug to feel high and a type of emotional warmth that creates a feeling of intimacy. It's become one of the most common illegal drugs sold on the streets, and it has caused many young people to end up in emergency rooms because of its dangerous side effects.

So, again, I ask, what is everyone trying to reach when they're high? I'm sure for young people experimenting, and even foolishly messing around with drugs like MDMA (ecstasy), it's because they just want to have a good time. But drugs, as we know, create a temporary high, and ecstasy in its most real form can visit us more frequently without having to pop a pill, snort a burning powder up our nose, or put, what can be, a lethal needle in our arm.

I've spoken about the natural "feel-good" chemicals in our brain, and what MDMA does is increase the activity of three brain chemicals: Dopamine, Norepinephrine, and Serotonin, which I described in my introduction.

All three of those chemicals increase energy, affect and elevate moods, as well as cause an emotional closeness the way MDMA does. Why we aren't tapping into our brain's natural ability to get us high is bewildering. Perhaps we're too Pavlovian for our own good, meaning when we condition ourselves to get pleasure from something like drugs, we go back for more, even if it's bad for us. Based on Russian Psychologist, Ivan Pavlov's theory that if you pair a "neutral stimulus," like a bell, with an "unconditioned stimulus," like food, it can produce an involuntary body response on its own. Pavlov observed while studying dogs, who, when conditioned, would salivate at the sound of the bell, knowing they would receive food.

Is it not time for us to condition our mind to think illumined thoughts so that we can trigger the feel-good chemicals in our brain, instead of relying on things outside of ourselves to satisfy us or get us high? I spoke about this in Chapter 5 - Divine Thought Illumination, and to repeat Alexander Scriabin's quote: "I am a moment illuminating eternity...I am affirmation...I am ecstasy."

When we are present, and free in our mind, we can let ecstasy visit us, and that is when we become "a moment illuminating eternity." I spoke about time standing still when we are in present moment awareness, and that is what is required of us to let ecstasy visit. If we free fall even further into the moment, we might be fortunate enough to have a mystical experience. Visits of ecstasy are glimpses of what it means to live life more aligned with the mystical, which, as we know, keeps us alive in awe and fascination. Why would we want to live any other way? As Charles Darwin said, "A man who dares waste one hour of time has not discovered the value of life."

The cosmic dance I spoke about is another magnificent way to connect to a feeling of ecstasy, and although the whole world is engaged in a grand cosmic dance, whether we are aware of it or not, it's our own individual interpretation of it that can inspire feelings of euphoria and bliss. Move your body whenever you can, and allow yourself to dance, even if it means by yourself. You may find yourself feeling a type of ecstasy that Sufi dancers experience in their whirling. It is said that the "ecstasy of dance" was created by mystic poet, Rumi. He had been walking towards a goldsmith and began dancing to the melodic sound of a hammer. He started whirling. It apparently made him so dizzy that he entered a trance, and became ecstatic. Sufi dancing is considered a spiritual practice, and just like the earth whirls around the sun, the goal is to achieve harmony with the universe itself.

And that's what ecstasy can do. It can put us in a trance of harmony with the universe, and we can get so high on life, we feel as though we are whirling through time and space. We truly are "illuminating eternity."

Ecstasy visits me
And tells me to
Never stop dancing
I am in a trance of
Harmony with the universe

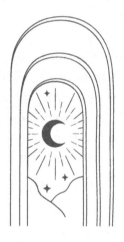

MINDFULNESS & MYSTICISM

MYSTICAL PERCEPTION

*Each person is at each moment capable of remembering all
that has ever happened to him and of perceiving everything
that is happening everywhere in the universe. The function
of the brain and nervous system is to protect us from being
overwhelmed and confused by this mass of largely useless and
irrelevant knowledge, by shutting out most of what we should
otherwise perceive or remember at any moment, and leaving
only that very small and special selection which is likely to be
practically useful.*

— ALDOUS HUXLEY

*Every beauty which is seen here by persons of perception
resembles more than anything else that celestial source from
which we all are come.*

— MICHELANGELO

*The moment you change your perception is the moment you
rewrite the chemistry of your body.*

— BRUCE LIPTON

Perception is an activity of the brain. Neuroscience tells us many things about the brain's functions and can explain the visual system, which perception is a part of, along with vision, hearing, taste, smell, and touch. But the part of perception that perhaps cannot be explained entirely through neuroscience is why the mind is perceiving something the way in which it is, in any given moment. On the research front, neuroscience is making great headway. But, there will be areas that might not easily be explained by science alone, and we must go further than exploring systems and structures of the brain. We must consider along with it, the workings of the soul, and its role in perception. Philosopher, Rene Descartes hypothesized that "we are able to see because the nerves project an object from the eyes into the brain, where it is perceived by the soul" (The National Library of Medicine). If that's the case, it doesn't seem that we can locate or pinpoint a part of the brain where the "spiritual or immaterial" part of us that is regarded as "immortal" exists.

If we go by Descartes' hypothesis that what we see is then perceived by the soul, mystical perception is seeing through our soul, as if it is a filter that separates what is real from what is not, and keeps our perceptions pure, and "in union with reality," which, as I've said, is non-separation from God, Divine presence, unity consciousness, oneness, or whatever you perceive as sacred or holy. When we perceive ourselves as separate from anything or anyone, that is when perception itself is distorted, and the mystical, or spiritual mystery of life is not perceivable.

And, if we subscribe to Dualism (I will go into this further in another chapter on nonduality), which is the belief that there are two kinds of reality, material (physical), and immaterial (spiritual), our perception of life will be constantly altered by which side of that reality we are engaging in, relating to, or at the effect of. Sometimes we are connecting to what we perceive as material/physical, and other times we are conscious of something identified as immaterial/spiritual, even though we don't spend as much time in that realm because we're not perceiving it as part of our daily life.

I feel the mystical experience is when there is no dualism perceived, and the physical and spiritual are joined together as one. That is when we are able to grasp mysticism as a natural state of consciousness. As I said, this is not a state we can be in all the time, but we certainly can experience it more if we recognize, as Pierre Teilhard de Chardin's quote says, "We are spiritual beings having a human experience." The more we understand this, and live our life not separate from the immaterial/spirit, the more our perception can be mystical, and this is when "Prima Facie" can be realized, which is a Latin term that means "at first sight" or "on its first encounter." What I mean by this is that we begin to perceive things mystically, and what we look at is seen in this way instantly.

This joins with Descartes' hypothesis that what we see is perceived through the soul, and if this is correct, it is our soul that yearns to connect to the mystical, which is why we mustn't think of ourselves as existing only in the material/physical. If the soul is considered non-physical, which it is often called, then we must ask ourselves how do we perceive the very thing that connects us to the mystical if not by our soul? As I said, we are much more comfortable with the material than that which is immaterial. We can relate to what we can see, or define as existing in the material realm. But, that takes us back to Sagan's quote, "We are made of star stuff." That means the "carbon, nitrogen, oxygen, and atoms in our bodies were created in previous generations of stars over 4.5 billion years ago," as he also said.

I know, that is probably not how you perceive yourself. Most people don't. We just don't think of ourselves as a bunch of atoms, but maybe if we did, we would be having a more natural relationship to the mystical, and it could be a magnificent one. We must ask ourselves, why do we feel more comfortable with only what we can see, or perceive as the material, and yet, what we long for is a spiritual experience or connection. This is why we seek God, or a Divine presence, for those of you who do. Churches and temples are filled with millions of people who go there to pray to a God or deity they believe in, and what many of them experience when they are in a receptive state to receive God's answers to their prayers is nothing short of mystical, or holy and sacred, as I described it. We seem to be fine with sensing, or experiencing the mystical if it comes to us in a place constructed for religious purposes. But once we take it out of a "holy place," we're right back to perceiving this world as a material reality, and there we go living in dualism all over again.

I understand how difficult it is to live in this mystical realm I'm writing about. I can't overstate how much I know that it is, and I too yearn to stay more in "union with reality" than disconnected from it. You see, this is the conundrum in which we exist. We are "spiritual beings having a human experience," or to take it even further, we are nothing more than the "carbon, nitrogen, oxygen, and atoms in our bodies that were created in previous generations of stars over 4.5 billion years ago," as Carl Sagan said. If that doesn't make us want to cling to the material to feel safe and secure, I don't know what will. I mean, think about it. We are made of "star stuff," and who wants to feel like we're floating in space like billions of stars? Does that even make sense? Maybe if you're an astrophysicist, and study something like a wormhole, a "hypothetical connection between widely separated regions of space-time," you accept things about the universe that might be hard or impossible for the average person to wrap their minds around. Most people are very comfortable with their "normal" or "ordinary" perceptions of the universe.

They hold onto the belief that there really isn't more for us to know other than what we already know.

Maybe we just have to be "out of the box" thinkers to believe in something that cannot necessarily be backed or explained by science alone, but still comfortable believing in what we cannot fully understand or even describe. And this is what the mystical does. It helps us glimpse into the invisible where we can experience something that can seem other worldly, or even ineffable. But we have to be okay with that. We have to know this, and trust that there is something greater than the "small self" that I spoke about in Chapter 12 - States of Consciousness.

And that "something greater" is more apparent to us when we look at life with a mystical perception of ourselves, the universe, and our role in it. But, we must develop this mystical perception like a skill that needs to be strengthened. If we are conscious of our perceptions, we can actually alter them; and instead of just looking at something, we really "see" it, as Thoreau suggested, and what we see includes both the material and the immaterial. Although we can't visibly see what is immaterial, we trust that it exists.

Let us explore our ability to use a mystical perception with a few exercises. One is for day, the other for night. You can do this with another person, or as many people as you like, but you need to be versed in guiding them.

Day:

1. Be somewhere out in nature.
2. Sit under a tree, walk on a beach, take a hike, etc.
3. As you are doing your outdoor activity, touch a piece of the earth with either your hands or feet, like the sand on a beach, water in the ocean, a tree, or rocks if you're hiking.
4. With your eyes either open or closed, imagine yourself absorbing or merging with the very thing you're feeling or touching.
5. Use your other senses too, like smell if you're smelling the ocean, or herbs in a garden, and taste if you're eating something from a tree like a berry or fruit. And if it's your sense of hearing, listen to all the sounds around you, like the ocean, animals, or insects.
6. Similar to the Cosmic Dance exercise, take a few deep breaths in and out, and connect to a place in your body that feels vital or sensual.
7. Imagine tremendous power, light, and heat coming from that place.
8. Let the energy you feel within guide you.
9. Allow yourself to transcend thought, and imagine you are guiding the universe in a way that feels free and uninhibited.
10. Feel your power, your strength, your freedom.
11. Surrender to the nature you're experiencing, and imagine you and it are "one." There is no separation.
12. Think of your spirit as eternal, and nature as something the spirit inhabits and becomes one with, once it leaves the body.
13. Think of yourself as a co-creator of the universe, spreading your love and light where you are, and everywhere.

Night:

1. Be outside where you can see the stars. It would be great if you can be somewhere where the stars are visible and exceptionally bright.
2. You can stand or lie down.
3. Let your eyes roam the night sky, taking in the magnitude of what you are seeing. If there is one star in particular that gets your attention, keep your focus on it.
4. Take a few deep breaths in and out.
5. Imagine the stars breathing in and out with you, and that you are one organism.
6. Continue doing this for a few minutes.
7. Imagine your spirit able to spring up from your body and join the stars, or one particular star, if that's where your attention is.
8. Consider yourself the observer of your spirit, and able to guide it to gently fly around the stars.
9. Imagine that your guidance of this is being directed from your third eye, which is the space between your brow. This is also known as the Pineal Gland, and refers to the place that leads to inner realms of higher consciousness.
10. Imagine that you and the stars are one. There is no separation.
11. Think of yourself as a co-creator of the universe, spreading your love and light throughout the cosmos.
12. When you are ready, bring your spirit back to your body. Take the time you need to transition out of this exercise.

Mystical perception allows us to see everything around us with non-dualism, meaning we don't consider ourselves separate from anything that we are experiencing through the "filter of our soul." This is something we can practice to help strengthen our ability to use a mystical perception with everything we are looking at. You can create your own exercises to use your mystical perception, and you may find yourself able to do it wherever you are, with whatever you are doing.

Sometimes I like to look into the sky at night, especially if it's a bright color, like pink, or a combination of orange and red, making it look like a blood orange. Apparently, the sun contains all of the colors of the rainbow in it, and when sunlight passes through certain particles in the air, it both refracts and reflects the light, which scatters some of the colors of the sunlight across the sky, and it can be absolutely beautiful. Occasionally, I've found myself transfixed on how unreal the sky looks, and I deliberately manipulate my perception of it, as if I am seeing it in a three-dimensional way. I have literally felt as if I can alter my "soul filter," like it's a type of camera lens a photographer would use, and zoom in or out. This not only changes the distance between me, the "seer," and the object (the sky) I am looking at, but makes me feel that I am also tapping into different levels of consciousness. "Cosmic consciousness," which, as I mentioned in Chapter 12 – States of Consciousness, is a higher form of consciousness than that possessed by the ordinary man.

Remember what I said about living an "ordinary life." We don't have to live our life that way if we choose to "apply our ordinary powers," as Newton said. That is when we transcend the ordinary and can even reach higher forms of consciousness that are not "possessed by the ordinary man." The goal is to use our mystical perception whenever we can so that we begin to live not only "less ordinary," but more in a state of non-duality, and that state can be quite euphoric, as if you and the blood orange sky have merged as one.

Meditation and contemplation can help prepare us to use our mystical perception by quieting the mind and allowing for non-doing, which makes for more receptivity to a feeling of oneness. Know that you have the ability to experience this life with a mystical perception, and when you begin to get comfortable with it, and use it more, you will find yourself living less on the first level of truth, meaning much less on the surface, or engaging on the superficial, but delving deeper into the multidimensionality of life. This is when veils begin to lift more frequently, and your perception will become not only much more enhanced, but you will know that it has been altered to that of the mystical, which can raise your consciousness to higher levels. Does that excite you? I hope so!

My perception
Is one of the mystical
I look beyond
The surface of things
And know
What lies beyond it
Is much more magical
I am not separate
From anyone
Or anything

MINDFULNESS & MYSTICISM

SPIRITUAL TRANSCENDENCE

An awake heart is like a sky that pours light.

— HAFIZ

Who would then deny that when I am sipping tea in my tearoom I am swallowing the whole universe with it and that this very moment of my lifting the bowl to my lips is eternity itself transcending time and space?

— DAISETZ TEITARO SUZUKI

Have you been able to feel more non-duality in your life? Are you experiencing more oneness? It's okay if you've only had glimpses of it, or even if you're just beginning to entertain the possibility of living your life differently, perhaps more transcendental. The more open you are to having mystical experiences, the more you will see your perception changing from the ordinary to the mystical. Remember, this can be very subtle. We mustn't disregard, or make light of even the slightest altering of our perceptions. This means it can be something as subtle as finding yourself more aware or attuned with how nature moves around you like the slow-motion movement of a branch bopping up and down on a tree, or the hypnotic rhythm of waves going in and out of the ocean and you find yourself feeling a type of bliss and contentment watching it. When we pay attention to these types of things all around us, which we more often than not take for granted, we can begin to notice how our perceptions are changing in ways that perhaps we weren't cognizant of before. Instead of waiting to "slip into a state of heightened awareness," which Jane Goodall experienced in a forest when she got "lost in awe at the beauty around me," we consciously seek out something awe-inspiring or mystical to happen to us by heightening our awareness on purpose.

The main thing is to stay open and receptive to mystical experiences, small or large. Personally, I like to deliberately use a "mystical perception" when I'm looking at certain things because I like the way it heightens my senses, and makes things appear more multidimensional. I shared how I have felt when I've looked at something like a blood orange sky, and experienced an altered perception because I stayed present and hyper-focused in the moment, which allowed me to "free fall" into the experience, and sharpen my "seeing" of it. Remember the quote I shared earlier by Thoreau: "It's not what you look at that matters, it's what you see." If we really want to experience a visionary state, which is the ability to get a clear picture of something that can seem or feel divine, we have to be fully present, and willing to hold ourselves very still in a moment so that we can connect with it in a way that feels completely whole and unified. This is what a mystical experience can feel like.

Another way in which I have deliberately used a mystical perception to heighten my senses is when there is a full moon. I consciously focus on the moon and recognize my non-separateness from it. Remember what I said before. If we acknowledge that we are not separate from anything or anyone, we can experience our inherent unity with all life, which includes the moon. When we are at one with nature, or the true nature of all things, it can create that feeling of oneness I've spoken about, and that is when we can feel a merging, a lovely melding of energies, both ours and the very thing we are feeling at one with. Again, this is exactly what a mystical experience can feel like.

When I do that, as I have when gazing at the full moon, before I know it, I am completely lost in the powerful energy emanating from the vibrant white glow of the full moon. As we know, the moon has held a mystical place in the history of human culture since the beginning of time. As Galileo said so simply, "It is a beautiful and delightful sight to behold the body of the Moon." And Joseph Conrad described it in even more stirring when he said, "There is something haunting in the light of the moon; it has all the dispassionateness of a disembodied soul, and something of its inconceivable mystery."

Again, if you think of your soul as the filter from which you see things, then anything you put your focus and awareness on can raise your perception higher, and that's when those "feel-good" chemicals in our brain start to kick in. We can, in fact, feel as if we're high in the same way we would on a mind-altering drug.

Here's the thing. You have probably had mystical experiences in your life and may not have known it, or you didn't know to call it that. That's what happened to me, as I've shared with you. And that's exactly what I'm aiming for. To bring that intoxicating feeling into our lives more often. Who wouldn't want to feel more delight or enchantment in their life? And we can. As I've said throughout this book, we can definitely have more magical and mystical experiences in our life naturally if we choose to, and why in the world wouldn't we choose to?

I know you want to or you wouldn't be reading my book. You decided to take this mystical journey with me, and I'm so glad you did! I say bring on more of the divine, and less of the mundane. Now, let's continue.

We're going to keep moving beyond the "small self," which I wrote about in Chapter 12 - States of Consciousness. I talked about "cosmic consciousness," which is going "beyond the small me" and can also be called "witness consciousness." You just experienced what that felt like in the previous chapter by doing mystical perception exercises. That can help you understand what it means to witness yourself in what you're doing. But, when you let go of the small self and merge with something greater than yourself, as I had you do with feeling your spirit dance with the stars, and be at one with the cosmos, that is when you can have a transcendental experience that goes way beyond the self that is preoccupied with mundane issues. You'd be amazed by how much time our minds spend thinking about small, trivial things when we could "trip the light fantastic," as I talked about in Chapter 14 - The Cosmic Dance. I asked if you were dancing the cosmic dance yet. That means you are free-falling into your most authentic self and living the cosmos in human form.

Remember, we are spiritual beings, lest we forget, so we must be mindful not to fall into the traps of the mundane, which not only fails to inspire our spirit to dance, but makes us feel that the cosmic dance is something that seems impossible to do. I don't like the word "impossible" and I'm asking you to begin removing it from your vocabulary or more than that, your mind entirely. Be mindful of what words fill that extraordinary mind of yours. Do not waste top real estate, as I like to call the vast, endless space of the thinking mind. It is yours to fill and curate whatever thoughts you choose, and why not make them transcendental? You might want to revisit Chapter 5 - Divine Thought Illumination. It's important to keep our thoughts illumined, which means "guided by light." If we keep the light on in our mind, and remain its gatekeeper, we can be that much more cognizant of when one of those sneaky, unwholesome, or dark thoughts starts to make its way into our psyche, and try to convince us that we should go along with what it's telling us. I don't think so! Stop right there unillumined thoughts! Not in my mind you go! That's what I want you to tell yourself. As I say in my first book, Says Who?, "You are the creator and master of your internal dialogue, which creates your reality."

How about creating a reality made up of spiritual transcendence? As D. T. Suzuki says in his quote above, who are we to deny that we are "swallowing the whole universe" as we sip our tea, and as we lift a bowl to our lips. It is "eternity itself transcending time and space." That's a great way to describe spiritual transcendence. You might be thinking, as I said before, "That's so out there!"

We are out there! Need I remind you that "we are made of star stuff," as Carl Sagan said. I've repeated this a few times, and hope you've warmed up to the idea of being a body full of atoms. The minute you stop forgetting that you are a "spiritual being having a human experience" you will continue to only focus on your basic human needs. If you only focus on that, spiritual transcendence won't seem likely for you.

You need to take breaks in your day from the stresses and demands of life. If you don't open the door in your mind for the mystical to visit you, then you're going to miss out on transcending the mundane, and that's how life can feel, mundane. What I mean by that is life can feel ordinary, uneventful, monotonous, or even disappointing, and that's usually when people need some kind of pick-me-up or escape, which is why they reach for alcohol and drugs, or spend endless hours on social media, which can be another form of addiction. Throughout this book, I'm proposing a type of transcendental high we can realize on this life journey. Even if you get glimpses of it, or wafts or whispers, you will know, and when you know, there is no turning back. You will say to yourself, "I know the mystical is always near me, and around me. And if at any time I doubt that there is a greater, more divine presence here with me, all I have to do is look in the mirror and see that I am a miracle created by this divine presence."

We just need to know and believe that it exists. And it does. This is how awakening happens. We open ourselves up to the transcendental truth of our existence, and that truth is we are connected to everything, both visible and invisible, material and spiritual. If we embrace this "union with reality" as Evelyn Underhill called the mystical so aptly, we are not pulled or conflicted by the dualism we may perceive, but instead alter our perception to include the mystical, which shows us the way of non-dualism.

Spiritual transcendence is having an awareness that we are not bound or limited by the opposing principles of the universe, which is light and dark, good and evil. If we keep our mind illumined by thoughts guided by light, we remain steadfast in our commitment to be the light in the darkness, the good in evil. We transcend all that is limiting or deceiving by remaining true to the spiritual nature of our being. Remember, our spirit can dance with the stars, for we are the cosmos in human form.

Spiritual transcendence

Rises above dualism

I am in its flow

Neither here

Nor there

But everywhere

MINDFULNESS & MYSTICISM

CHAPTER 23

MYSTICISM AND CREATIVITY

*The heart of creativity is an experience of the mystical union;
the heart of the mystical union is an experience of creativity.*

— JULIA CAMERON

*The new meaning of soul is creativity and mysticism.
These will become the new psychological type and with him or
her will come the new civilization.*

— OTTO RANK

*The mystical experience is doubly valuable; it is valuable
because it gives the experiencer a better understanding of
himself and the world and because it may help him to lead a
less self-centered and more creative life.*

— ALDOUS HUXLEY

Poet T.S. Eliot called inspiration "the mystical quality of creativity," which makes you wonder what makes it mystical. By knowing the answer to that, can it tell us where inspiration comes from?

When we speak of the mystical as "invisible" or "transcendent," we may not get an answer for either question, but I want to explore the connection of mysticism and creativity. As we delve further into that connection, we may discover along the way where inspiration comes from, which might take us closer to knowing more about how creativity gets ignited.

One of the definitions of inspiration is "a divine influence or action on a person believed to qualify him or her to receive and communicate sacred revelation." This brings us back to what I spoke about in Chapter 5 - Divine Thought Illumination, when Saint Augustine said, "The mind needs to be enlightened by light from outside itself." If that's true, where does this light come from? Augustine felt it was from God, which he explains when he says, "You will light my lamp, Lord. You hear nothing true from me which you have not first told me."

Could this be where inspiration comes from; the lamp that is lit by God? In that chapter I also spoke about "supernatural assistance," and proposed the following question: "Do we need to be helped in order to experience divine illumination?" If we ask for help from God, or a Divine source, we may very well receive it if, first and foremost, we are open to receiving it and believe that we will. Do we know for certain that it is God, or a Divine presence that has answered our prayer or request? What is certain is what we believe, and what we believe is personal. As I said in Chapter 6 - Living a Divine Life, "If you are open to living a life of heightened awareness; a state of mind that Jane Goodall felt she 'slipped into' that caused her to experience 'the moment of truth' that suddenly came upon her, then you are likely to experience more divinity in your life."

When it comes to creativity, however, we know that many artists get blocked in their artistry. If it were that easy to call upon God, or a Divine presence to ignite it, we would have many more artists telling us about it instead of hearing about "writer's block," or losing the ability to produce new work. There is nothing worse for an artist than feeling blocked or uninspired creatively. This can literally cause them to go into a state of depression and believe that their creative well has dried up. And it certainly can feel that way when creativity eludes us, which I feel is caused primarily by the stagnant, or low energy of our spirit because of a lack of tending to its needs, as I spoke about in Chapter 16 - The Human Spirit. We are unable to call forth inspiration of any kind.

This isn't just a problem artists face. Our soul yearns for creative expression, whether you're an artist or not, and each of us, in our own way, is. As author Don Miguel Ruiz said, "Every human is an artist. And this is the main art that we have: the creation of our story." And what do we wish our story to be? This is where the mystical comes in, whether you're an actual artist or not. We each have a story to tell, whether we tell it in a book, on a canvas, or by composing a piece of music. Why not tell it ignited by divine inspiration?

But can we ignite it ourselves, or do we need help? It depends. Some people are able to tap into some kind of powerful energy source for stimulation and motivation to get their creative juices going, and for others they wait for the magic to come to them. As I say in my book, Live True, "Real magic comes from within. Yes, there's outside magic like sunsets, rainbows, and eclipses, as well as many magical places and mystical lands. The world is full of magical places like the Taj Mahal, the Grand Canyon, or the Sorcerer's Castle in Switzerland, to name a few, and you can travel to see that kind of magic whenever you want to. But, what do you do when you can't go to the magic, and want the magic to come to you? That's when you turn to the magic within you. You sit quietly, breathe, and go within to the most magical place of all, yourself. This is the first step of practicing Mindfulness, a practice that will allow you to access The Magic Within whenever you desire."

And yet, even though the magic is within you, you must stay open and in a state of heightened awareness. This magic is yours to experience. Could this be how we jumpstart inspiration, which is the "mystical quality of creativity," of which T.S. Eliot spoke of? Perhaps this can also occur when we do nothing, and the mystical experience happens unexpectedly, but what we know is that there is an openness, a readiness to receive something magical. What we can feel at the core of our being is a blast of inspiration, which then enables us to realize "a divine influence or action" that can qualify us to "receive and communicate sacred revelation," as inspiration has been defined. These mystical experiences can ignite our soul, which not only has the power to transform our life, but can also spark our creativity to such a degree, there's no limit to what can be created.

Could a masterpiece like the ceiling of the Sistine Chapel painted by Michelangelo have been done by receiving divine inspiration? And even though it was painted at the commission of Pope Julius II, was Michelangelo's creativity ignited by something incomprehensible to the human mind? Did God light his lamp and gift him limitless inspiration to make this masterpiece possible?

In ancient times, the Greeks believed that the artist would go into "ecstasy" and be "transported beyond their own mind, and given the gods' or goddesses' own thoughts to embody." And, in Christianity, inspiration is believed to be a "gift of the Holy Spirit," as well as considered a "divine matter" in Hebrew poetics. If we go by the definition of inspiration I mentioned, "a divine influence or action on a person believed to qualify him or her to receive and communicate sacred revelation," then apparently revelation is a "conscious process." This means we are aware that we are receiving this "gift," be it of the "Holy Spirit," or a divine source of our understanding. But what's interesting about inspiration is that it is considered "involuntary" and can be received without an understanding as to why we're receiving it.

So, how do we become inspired if it happens "without will or conscious control"? We cannot demand to receive inspiration any more than we can insist on having a mystical experience, which I spoke about in Chapter 7 - Self Surrender. I quoted Terence McKenna saying we cannot expect a mystical experience to "perform on demand the way psychedelics do because that would be essentially man ordering God at man's whim, which is not how it's supposed to work." I went on to say, "No, we cannot order God at our whim, no more than we can order having a mystical experience. If we truly want to connect to something greater than who we think we must be in order to feel worthy or important, we must relinquish the false self that stands in the way of our readiness to receive a greater knowing of who we are, which is much more than our identity or persona. When we are connected to the divine, and let ourselves live it daily, the mystical will find its way to us, but we must surrender, and keep surrendering until we are brought to our knees with humility and gratitude for this miraculous journey we are on."

Here is a meditation to open yourself to receive creative inspiration. Again, this is not something we can "demand." Instead, we are allowing for a "divine influence" to come forward.

1. Find a quiet place to sit.
2. Close your eyes.
3. Take a few deep breaths in and out.
4. Say silently, "I am surrendered to my authentic self."
5. Say silently, "My creativity lives in the truth of my soul."
6. Say silently, "I am open for a divine influence to come forward."
7. Say silently, "I am ready for the mystical union of creativity to take place."
8. Imagine an energy of inspiration rushing through you like a bolt of electric light.
9. When you are ready, open your eyes.

As I said, one of the reasons our creativity can elude us is because of a stagnant, or low energy of our spirit, and if we are not tending to its needs, it's very difficult to call forth inspiration of any kind. It's also very important to be mindful of staying connected to the true expression of our creativity, which stems from the authentic self. If we want to feel inspired to optimize our creativity, we must let go of any false ideas or illusions of who we are, so that our most authentic self can keep us open and ready to receive inspiration that can ignite our unique form of creativity. Essentially, we must get out of our own way and not block ourselves from the creative process. We may call it "writer's block" when we are unable to create a piece of written work, but where do we think the block is coming from? Do not wait to get unblocked, or inspired, but avail yourself to the inspiration that can ignite you. Stay open to what you may receive, and if it's a "sacred revelation" that is given to you, and you are fortunate to find yourself in a state of "ecstasy," surrender to it, and let it take you beyond the limitations of your mind where you might have believed that a block is real. No, a block is a self-imposed belief that you cannot receive something "holy" or "divine." You most certainly can, and when you do, you will know because it will feel like a powerful burst of energy is suddenly moving through you, and awakening every cell of your being. Was It God? A Divine presence? You can decide.

Why don't we leave it with this quote by Rumi: "Although you appear in earthly form your essence is pure consciousness. You are the fearless guardian of Divine Light."

I am an open vessel

From which creativity

Can pour through me

And from there

Creativity knows

No bounds

MINDFULNESS & MYSTICISM

CHAPTER 24

SUPERNATURAL POWERS

What is there unreasonable in admitting the intervention of a supernatural power in the most ordinary circumstances of life?

— JULES VERNE

The beginning of wisdom is the beginning of supernatural power.

— PARACELSUS

Through systematic exercising of our thinking faculties, we can train ourselves for exact clairvoyance. Imaginative Knowledge is the first step in supersensible perception, and through it we reach the first element of the supersensible it is possible to reach, namely, the supersensible body that we bear within our earthly body in physical space.

— RUDOLF STEINER

When we think of who possesses supernatural powers, what comes to mind are mythical figures, Gods and Goddesses, or comic book heroes. Mere mortal beings don't "leap tall buildings in a single bound" like Superman does, or "move faster than a speeding bullet," or are "more powerful than a locomotive."

We go to movies to see these types of superheroes do the things we wish we could do. We get a vicarious thrill because we, too, want to be super human and have supernatural powers which we do.

Okay, we may not be able to "leap tall buildings" or do any of the things Superman can, but we definitely have supernatural powers, which we may be unaware we possess. If we're not aware of the powers we have then how can we possibly use them?

Our greatest superpower is the power of our mind. It is the source from which all feats can be performed. If we are guided by what it tells us, we can act on it, and what we can do can be considered "supernatural." One of the definitions of supernatural is as follows: "Behavior supposedly caused by the intervention of supernatural beings." This book is intended to take the focus off what exists outside of ourselves, and put it on who we are, and what we are capable of, which I've said is quite extraordinary. As you can tell from what you've read so far, I don't discount external powers that can influence us, but I will continue to focus on our own abilities, and what we can access from within. What help we get from outside, or "above," is like getting extra offerings from the universe, as far as I'm concerned. This is a great big cosmic playground we exist in, and the more expansive we are, the more we can experience all of the magic it has to offer, and join it together with our own.

But we also need to know that we have innate, natural powers that can be considered supernatural, paranormal, transcendent, metaphysical, or even "other worldly." We all have the ability to transcend our "humanness" and be guided more by our spirit, and, as I've said about the spirit, it is with us all of the time. Our spirit is the conduit from where we can be in "contact" with whatever we choose, be it supernatural or transcendent. We house our spirit in our body. It is the vehicle it inhabits. And, if we tend to our spirit, as I've suggested we do daily, we can live more connected to what is "heavenly" or mystical, and this helps us access our supernatural powers. We don't have to be weighed down by our "earthly" tendencies and needs, but as I mentioned earlier, that doesn't mean we have to be floating ten feet off the ground. No, we can be very rooted on this earth, and also be an open, receptive channel for our spirit to flow, and "receive" offerings from the universe, which can inspire our creativity. This is your movie, and you can manifest it to be exactly what you want it to be. I said let's make it less "mundane" and more mystical, and we can do that by recognizing our supernatural powers.

Here are some powers you may have that can be considered supernatural:

1. Clairvoyance – The ability to see the unknown.
2. Telepathy – The power to read people's minds.
3. Mediumship – Mediating communication between spirits of the dead and living human beings.
4. Remote viewing – The power to track people or objects from afar.
5. Precognition – The ability to see the future.
6. Enhanced Memory – The ability to recall any memory.
7. Psychometry – The ability to read information from objects that belonged to someone.
8. Astral Projection – The ability to separate from the physical body and travel somewhere else.
9. Telekinesis – The ability to move things with one's mind.

You might read this list and identify with something on it, or you might think something like, "My grandmother saw spirits," or "I've been to psychics, and they have the ability to see the future," or "I've had dreams where I flew around the room, but didn't know what that was." Many of us have had feelings, sensations, or experiences that felt or seemed unusual, even "other worldly," and we either accepted it, went with it, feared it, or didn't know what it was so we didn't give it much thought, and maybe even forgot about it. This is what I've also said about the mystical experience. You may have had one, but didn't know what it was.

These experiences are usually fleeting, and even if they last a moment, we can, as Underhill said, "catch it" and if we do, "it is so real that to look upon it as wrong would be an unthinkable absurdity." Supernatural powers, as well as mystical experiences, don't need to be thought of as unusual, strange, esoteric, or something only "other people" experience, and not us. We can experience pretty much anything we want to, and if we want to venture a little more in the direction of what could be called "extramundane," meaning outside, or beyond the "physical realm," we can.

When people describe something like having an "out of body experience," what that means is they experienced a sensation outside their body, and saw themselves floating above it; watching what was happening like an observer. And, for anyone who has had such an experience, it's usually when something life-threatening happened, or they were on the verge of death, and what they describe most often is that they felt very peaceful.

Do we need to be on the verge of something life threatening, or the possibility of death to experience the extraordinary or miraculous? Can we not be fully present and open to experience special, mystical, magical, or miraculous moments, and not necessarily be floating above our body to have them? Our spirit can hover over our body, which some people have felt in a dream state, or experience something called astral projection, as I mentioned in the list of supernatural powers, which is "an intentional out of body experience where the soul or consciousness separates from the physical body and is capable of travelling outside it throughout the universe," as it is described, but again, one doesn't need to be in a life-threatening situation for it to happen. And the kind of peacefulness people have described when they were having an out of body experience could be because the weightiness of our earthly desires, needs, and expectations are burdensome for us. We might not know this until we're on the verge of death, but again, why wait to be at death's door to feel such a lightness of being.

The idea is to lighten our load a bit more on this life journey, which, as I said can feel burdensome and weighty, and for some people it can affect them to such a serious degree they feel that life is not enjoyable, but instead, miserable. What if you are one of those people who isn't exactly enamored with life, and find it anything but magical or mystical? And what if you were told you have a supernatural power? You might laugh and think that's ridiculous, or you might be curious to find out what your supernatural power is. Remember what I said earlier: Mindfulness can be considered a type of superpower, and when practiced consistently and strengthened, I believe it can be the gateway to developing a supernatural power. It doesn't mean it can guarantee that you can move an object across a table, but one does need to be fully present, and have a heightened sense of awareness to concentrate deeply, to perform a mental power like that if you believe it's possible. I feel that Mindfulness is at the root of every supernatural power and psychic ability, be it clairvoyance, or mediumship, and enables us to alter our perceptions in present time, which means we can expand our limited perception of reality. That's when you can perform something that seems paranormal, or "beyond the scope of normal scientific understanding."

Some people feel that their supernatural power, or what can also be called a "gift," found them, and there are stories of it happening when they were at a very low point in their life. Acclaimed medium, Rebecca Rosen, was a college student struggling with depression and a debilitating sleep and eating disorder. After months of therapy and medication, she began to pray. One day while she was writing in her journal, her deceased grandmother "Babe" answered her prayers. She found herself channeling, and involuntarily transcribing words in her journal, which she felt was her grandmother speaking to her. At first skeptical, Rebecca asked her grandmother for proof that what she was experiencing was real. Apparently, her grandmother told her three specific things to share with her family, which turned out to be true. "Grandma Babe" became Rebecca's guide, and she told Rebecca to "fulfill her life's purpose, and help others," which she has done for thousands of people as a medium. She helped me at a time when I was grieving, and in deep mourning over the passing of my brother, Daniel. She gave me a reading over the phone, and it was nothing short of amazing. Her ability to mediate communication with his spirit at the time of his death helped me know that all of the mystical things I was experiencing was him communicating with me, even though he was no longer in his body. I have no doubt that the spirit continues on once it sheds the body; the vehicle it inhabited for as long as it did and if you're open to communicating with the spirit of a loved one, you most certainly can.

Rebecca is one example of someone who was at a very low point in their life, and through prayer, asked for guidance and received it. Prayer can be extremely power-ful, and when we connect to a deep place within us, and ask for help, we are actually opening ourselves to receive a mystical experience, which I consider Rebecca Rosen's visit from her "Grandma Babe" to be. Our "lamp can be lit," and whether it's God, your deceased grandmother, or something that cannot be put into words, when you are ready for something to "meet you," and by that, I mean re-ceive something that meets your spirit and lifts it up and lets it soar, you will feel it and know.

Another person who is considered to possess super-powers is Wim Hof, also known as the "iceman." He is able to withstand extreme cold temperatures, and "holds twenty-one Guinness World Records including a world record for the longest ice bath." He describes his ability to withstand extreme cold temperatures as being able to "turn his own thermostat up" by using his mind.

Yes, it is the mind that is our greatest superpower. How we choose to use it can help determine what we can turn on or "up" in our body, which then enables us to withstand things that might seem like only a comic book hero can tolerate.

Why don't we begin with the belief that we can tap into our "supernatural" abilities, whatever that means or looks like for us. We don't need to declare ourselves as superhuman; we simply acknowledge ourselves as being very human, and in our humanness, we are capable of extraordinary things. Supernatural comes from the Latin word supernaturalis, which means "beyond nature" and "caused by something that can't be explained by the laws of nature." If we need to explain every unusual or mystical thing we can experience, or have experienced as being something that is "beyond nature," or "beyond the range of man's perceptions," then we are taking ourselves out of the equation of how the mystical happens, or what possessing supernatural powers means.

Yes, it may seem that we are going "beyond the known" when mystical or supernatural things happen, but once we enter into the "unknown," it becomes known to us. We realize how aligned with our true nature those experiences really are. The mystical and the supernatural are in the range of "man's perceptions" but we just need to be able to see what can seem invisible to us.

Again, I want to remind you of an inherent power you have, which when used properly, can be the basis for developing supernatural powers and that's Mindfulness. Here's what I said about it in Chapter 1 - Behold Mindfulness: "When you do use it, it strengthens, and the more you use it, you get to take full advantage of the abundant, even mystical and transcendent gifts it can bring into your life. Mindfulness, when practiced consistently, can feel like your awareness is so laser sharp, that you can see things beyond what's on the surface. And that's when the invisible can become visible for us because we are looking beyond what is only on the surface."

When we increase the practice of Mindfulness, we continue to heighten our awareness so that we can be better prepared to experience the mystical. If we do things like open ourselves up so that we can be in a state of receptivity, we can receive the information or guidance to know what other supernatural powers we may have. That's when we can come to know the "gifts" that might lie dormant in us, the way Rebecca Rosen came to know hers. If we ask, we "shall receive" precious information that can be life changing, but we must be present and fully aware to know what it is we are asking for, and why.

Here is a meditation you can do to connect to a supernatural power or gift:

1. Find a quiet place to sit.
2. Close your eyes.
3. Take a few deep breaths in and out.
4. Say silently, "I am an open channel."
5. Say silently, "My spirit is here to guide me."
6. Say silently, "What supernatural power or gift do I possess?"
7. Allow for whatever thought, or image to come to your mind. Accept it with non-judgment. You might hear a voice say: "heal" or "guide" or "lead." You might see yourself as a healer, shaman, medium acupuncturist, therapist, or wellness practitioner.
8. You might see yourself as a creative: writer, painter, musician.
9. Note how your thought or image makes you feel. Simply observe it.
10. Say silently, "I am ready to be shown the way of my superpower or gift".
11. When you are ready, open your eyes.
12. Take the time you need to transition out of your meditation.

So, how can you live your life more supernaturally, or with a more heightened awareness of your superpowers, which you may not know you have? Begin with being as present as you possibly can in each moment, and stay receptive to "knowing more." You might have an inkling that you are capable of some supernatural abilities like some of the ones I mentioned above, but you haven't allowed yourself to explore or develop them more. Whether you're aware of your superpowers, or you'd like to delve deeper into exploring the possibility of having the ability to do something like be a medium, or use your mind as powerfully as Wim Hof does, you can begin exploring your gifts, superpowers, and supernatural powers at any time. Does it mean you have to live your life any differently than you are right now? No, it does not. What it does mean is that you are unafraid to know what might not be able to be fully explained, things that seem "beyond nature."

But is it? Is the mystical or a supernatural power, beyond nature? Perhaps, but isn't that what beckons us to go beyond what we may not see or know? And when we do "know," we understand the mystery of what we hadn't known before. It is there we can meet not only our superpowers but perhaps a supernatural power we possess, which has been there all along waiting for us to know it.

I have
Supernatural powers
They are my gifts
My treasures
Waiting for me
To discover them

MINDFULNESS & MYSTICISM

CHAPTER 25

COMMUNION WITH THE INVISIBLE

The deepest level of communication is not communication, but communion. It is wordless ... beyond speech ... beyond concept.

— THOMAS MERTON

If it is "daily bread," why do you take it once a year? ... Take daily what is to profit you daily. Live in such a way that you may deserve to receive it daily. He who does not deserve to receive it daily, does not deserve to receive it once a year.

— ST. AMBROSE OF MILAN

Wisdom is a sacred communion.

— VICTOR HUGO

Spiritual Communion is a Christian practice of "desiring union with Jesus Christ." St. Thomas Aquinas defined it as having an "ardent desire to receive Jesus Christ in the Holy Sacrament" which is a "religious ceremony or ritual" where one receives God's love (or forgiveness of sins if you are religious) either by baptism, blessing, or anointment.

I consider myself a spiritual person, not a religious one, and when a religion goes into areas with which I am unfamiliar, I look for what is most resonant to my soul, rather than focusing on religious dogma or beliefs. As far as "spiritual communion" is concerned, I'm going to use its meaning, not in a religious context, but as having a desire to be in union with a Divine presence, be it God, Christ, or whatever holds sacred meaning for you. This spiritual communion is something anyone can experience, religious or not.

I believe that we all want to be in communion with some type of Divine presence, whatever that might be. When we embark on the path of mysticism, we seek to be in union with the Divine, and to remain in union with it always. Because Spiritual Communion is thought of as a religious practice, and it has been a part of Catholic life for centuries, I propose the question, as I did earlier, about a mystical experience, which is, does one have to be religious to experience it? I don't believe so. I want to bridge the gap between religious differences or beliefs, and instead, join with what unites us. If we have a desire

to feel God's embrace, or the embrace of the Divine upon
us, then our desires are the same. We needn't let religion
separate us, as it historically has done since the beginning
of time. Unfortunately, religion has caused more wars
than it has peace, and even in the 21st century, we are
still struggling with religious intolerance, which basically
means the unwillingness to put up with someone else's
beliefs.

But, as I said earlier, I don't want to veer off into
religion. Instead, I want to stay focused on our soul, and
what we hold deep in it. I said the following in Chapter
5 - Divine Thought Illumination:

"I'm not concerned with how you find, or access your
light, and is it really any of our business which religious,
or non-religious well anyone drinks from to quench their
soul's thirst for a greater, or more sacred meaning of this
life?" Having a thirst for a greater meaning is what keeps
us open to receive a deeper understanding of this life, and
it is in our receiving that we can take in whoever or whatever is sacred or holy for us be it God, Christ, or whatever
the Divine means to us.

The beauty of communion comes from its literal
meaning, which is "sharing" and "breaking bread together." If we bring one another into the home of our heart,
we can share a holiness that unites us because each of us
has a heart to bring one another into. And, if we keep that
holiness nameless, but instead think of it as the invisible,

that which does not need to be named or labeled, we can take communion together at any time, and with anyone, no matter their religious, or non-religious beliefs.

So what type of "sacrament" can we experience to receive the blessing that is given to someone who is ready to be graced by God, Christ, or a manifestation of the Divine that holds no name? What ceremony or rite of passage do we need to go through for our soul to be ready to take in the love of God, Christ, or a nameless manifestation of the Divine? And what oath must we take so that we can achieve purification and regeneration to be admitted into the house of God?

The mystical doesn't ask us to take oaths, but what it does do is ask us to trust our heart and soul, and keep them always open to receive something that can be called holy, spiritual, transcendental, supernatural, or even religious to describe your entry into the Divine. When we keep ourselves open to be "energized by the invisible," as Evelyn Underhill called the mystical, we no longer need to "rest in the mere enjoyment of the visible."

Communion with the invisible means that your heart is open to receive the gifts or blessings that can be given to you by a divine, holy, or sacred presence or being, even if you can't see who or what it is in physical form. And, if you happen to gaze your eyes on a manifestation of the Divine such as an image of Christ, a deity, or religious figure that resonates for you, you can feel yourself taken into their embrace, and feel their love upon you, whether you are religious or not.

Being embraced or loved by a religious manifestation of the Divine should not be determined by your belief or worship of it. How we choose to be received, seen, loved, blessed, or even forgiven is based on our own private relationship to something we deem as sacred. We must stop comparing what is more or most sacred, and leave each other alone to respect, love, or even worship who or what we believe is holy. We must ask ourselves, "What does my God have to do with you?" or "What does my God want or need from you?" or perhaps, more importantly, "Does my God want me to judge, love you less, or even hate you because you do not love or worship them?"

I prefer that you invite me into the home of your heart, as I will invite you into mine, and we can break bread with one another from a place of love and acceptance. Wouldn't it be magnificent if we could travel the world and invite one another into the millions of hearts that live on this planet, and together we can share our own experience of communion, whatever that might be? We can then tell our stories of what the Divine means to us, and describe what might be invisible so that we can hold those divine images in our minds collectively. That's how the invisible becomes visible, by how we bring ourselves, and one another, into a "union with reality," which is knowing that we are not separate from each other, and all that exists.

Can you trust the invisible? Do you feel confident that you can open yourself up to what you cannot see but are ready to experience? Do you wish to experience your own version of the sacrament, whatever that might be for you? What is your personal practice or ritual to receive blessings from a Divine source so that you can feel embraced and loved by something that moves your soul deeply?

Let me give you a meditation to be in communion with the invisible. You can do this anywhere and at any time, and it needn't be religious. And if you are, consider this meditation as taking your church, temple, mosque, or holy place of worship with you wherever you go. All you have to do is sit somewhere quiet, close your eyes, and imagine the invisible.

1. Sit somewhere quiet.
2. Close your eyes.
3. Take a few deep breaths in and out.
4. If your mind begins to wander, simply put your focus and awareness back onto your breath.
5. Say silently, "I am open to receive love from the Divine.
6. Say silently, "Embrace me in your light and love."
7. Say silently, "My heart and soul are filled with the light and love of which you give me."
8. Imagine light and love filling every part of your being.
9. See it as a vibrant, white light that is igniting every cell in your body.
10. Feel the warmth and radiance of the light and love that is moving through your body.
11. When you are ready, open your eyes.
12. Take as much time as you need to transition out of your meditation.

Whether you are in a house of worship, or not, you are always in the home of your heart. Know that you can bring yourself into this sacred place that dwells within you whenever you choose to, and also know that you can invite anyone into the home of your heart too, no matter their spiritual or religious beliefs. Sit quietly each day so that you can feel the warmth of a Divine presence embrace you. This is communion with the invisible, and this communion is possible always. Remember: You are holy, you are pure, you are worthy, and you are always ready to receive and be filled with Divine light and love.

I invite you into

The home of my heart

It is a sacred dwelling place

Where the Divine dwells with me

Let us break bread together

And drink the wine of the Gods

Of which there are many

Visible and invisible

MINDFULNESS & MYSTICISM

CHAPTER 26

PROTECTING THE SACRED

To the poet, to the philosopher, to the saint,
all things are friendly and sacred, all events
profitable, all days holy, all men divine.

— RALPH WALDO EMERSON

In this moment, everything is sacred.

— ARIEL

In the previous chapter, I said that "communion with the invisible means that you are open to receive the gifts or blessings that can be given to you by a divine, holy, or sacred presence or being, even if you can't see who or what it is in physical form, which is what a mystical experience can be like. Remember, you can have a holy or sacred experience whether you're in a temple, church or mosque, or, as Rumi said, you can find the divine "within your heart." Sacredness is all around us. We just need to see it, and trust that it is there.

But, there are people who don't feel connected to something sacred. For many, life is to be lived believing that there is nothing to be known of the existence or nature of God that "goes beyond material phenomena," as Agnostics believe. I view that as meaning if you can't see God, or there is no proof that a God exists, there isn't one.

The Hebrew word for holy is "qodesh," and it means "apartness," "separateness," and also "otherness." That implies that something sacred and holy, like God, is separate from us because He is "above his creation."

If God is considered a "totally other," and you don't believe there is an "other," especially a holy other, then it would seem reasonable that you have no need to revere, worship or feel devotional towards something that may universally, or archetypally, be regarded as God, or God-like.

There are millions of people who live as "non-believers," meaning they don't believe in God, but that doesn't mean they don't feel connected to something that can be described as sacred. As I mentioned before, some people are religious, and others are spiritual. I am a spiritual seeker. I love nothing more than to ponder the meaning of life, and explore the mystery of it, that which we may not see. This is the mystical of which I speak, which can be, as I said, both visible and invisible. All of it, I feel, is sacred.

It is when we do not view life, or the mystery of it, as sacred that we are not open to being "energized by the invisible," as Evelyn Underhill described the mystical experience. If you feel that you are separate from the sacred, you not only lose sight of its greater meaning, but you also fail to allow yourself to experience something that needn't be confused with God, worship, or devotion. You can see how the mystical and religion have been perceived as synonymous over the centuries. I feel there can be a genuine confusion, or a perpetuated belief that in order to have a sacred or holy experience, it must be religious. This is not so, and as I've talked about, many people have had a mystical experience, which felt sacred to them, and they themselves were not religious or necessarily believed in God.

What you need to ask yourself is whether you believe in something that is sacred, and if so, what does sacred mean to you? What does it look like? If we only regard God, or something God-like as sacred, then it might be difficult to hold the idea of sacredness as something to believe in and revere that isn't as holy as God or a God-like entity. There are so many things that can be considered sacred, and that can mean something you have great respect or awe for, or moves your soul deeply, and again, it may or might not be religious.

Some examples of what could be considered sacred are as follows:

1. **Love** – This means that we hold love as sacred and recognize that genuine love comes from a deep spiritual, mystical, and energetic connection.

2. **Marriage** – The union of two people joined in matrimony is a sacred one. It is considered a covenant, and when we enter this union, we vow to honor and respect one another during all phases of this union, which includes "in sickness and in health." The sacredness of this union goes beyond the contractual and the physical, and upon entering the marriage bond, it is agreed that the divine nature of two beings are joined together to walk the path of transformation and awakening.

3. **Childbirth** – Bringing a child into this world is sacred, and each new being that enters this earth plane

is part of a divine plan to raise consciousness. With each new soul that is born, it is an opportunity for more love and light to spread throughout the universe.

4. **The Earth** – Our planet Earth is sacred, and worthy of our highest regard. The word "Gaia" is the name of the ancient Greek goddess of the Earth, and the Incas call her Pachamama. She is the creator of all life, and we are meant to honor and respect her. We have failed terribly at this made evident by the pollution of her seas, and the severe climate disruption we're experiencing. That does not mean we cannot come to her aid and revive her, which millions of people all over the world are actively doing by participating in things like unplugging our devices more, recycling, omitting the use of plastic, embracing a minimalist lifestyle, and reducing our carbon footprint. Buying locally-sourced, organic, plant-based, or unprocessed food from local farmers are other ways to help sustain the well-being of the Earth. You can see there is much we can do to regard "Mama Earth" as sacred, which she most certainly is.

5. **Animals** – All sentient beings are sacred, including animals. "Sentience" means "the ability to feel, perceive, or be conscious," so I think it's fair to say that animals fall into that category, and therefore should be considered as sacred as human beings. Animals are

mentioned throughout the Bible. "The seventh day is a sabbath to the Lord your God; in it you shall not do any work, you, or your son, or your ox, or your ass, or any of your cattle" (Exodus 23:12) and, "Ask the animals, and they will teach you, or the birds in the sky, and they will tell you, or speak to the earth, and it will teach you, or let the fish in the sea inform you. Which of all of these does not know that the hand of the Lord has done this? In His hand is the life of every creature and the breath of all mankind" (Job 12:7-10).

I also find it interesting that dog spelled backwards is God. Coincidence? Maybe it's a reminder to treat a dog as a sacred being, just as we would like to be treated, yes? This lovely quote by Jane Goodall adds to the sacredness of animals: "We should have respect for animals because it makes better human beings of us all."

6. **Temples, Churches, Mosques** – These consecrated places are sacred because this is where millions of people go to pray, worship, study, and congregate to perform acts of devotion to the God or Goddess of their belief. Each place, or house of worship has different rituals depending on the religion, and how that religion honors God, (Goddess), Christ, or the Lord of that particular faith. Some of those structures, like the Parthenon in Athens remained sacred for many centuries. Built for the Goddess Athena in 447-432 BC, it remained devoted to her cult for nearly

a thousand years. Later, it became a Christian church, and then an Islamic Mosque under the Ottoman Empire. The Parthenon was significantly damaged when the Venetians, led by Francesco Morosini, attacked Athens, but it remains one of the most popular historical sites in the world. The history of these places is what keeps the sacredness alive, and for many people who visit them, they feel they can imbibe the sacredness as if time stands still, and they are transported back to when these sacred places were occupied. This is how the mystical experience can feel, as if past, present, and future are like a space-time continuum, and we are travelling the multiple dimensions of time and space simultaneously. There are many other sacred places we can visit throughout the world that hold deep meaning for many when they go there. Places like the Church of the Holy Sepulchre in Jerusalem, which is considered one of the most sacred shrines in Christianity. It is visited by millions of people from all over the world throughout the year since it was founded in 326 AD. Many Christians believe it was built on the site of Jesus' Crucifixion and burial, and where He rose again from the dead. I visited it, and I can say that the mystical energy there was palpable. Time definitely felt as if it stood still. Other historical places that are considered sacred today include the Kashi Vishwanath Temple in India, which is dedicated to Lord Shiva, who is believed to have appeared there as a "fiery column of light." Another sacred site in

India is the Mahabodhi Temple in Bodh Gaya, Bihar. Completed in the 7th Century to commemorate Prince Siddhartha Gautama's enlightenment, it is the most sacred place of pilgrimage for the Buddhists in the world. Lourdes in France, another place of pilgrimage, gained attention and fame amongst Catholics in 1858 when the Virgin Mary was believed to have appeared eighteen times to a local fourteen-year-old girl, Bernadette Soubrious. Was she having a mystical experience? You decide. Another major sacred site to mention is Mount Sinai, Egypt, which is extremely important to the Jewish, Christian, and Islamic faiths, and believed by many to be where Moses received the 10 commandments from God. It is said that saints, prophets, pilgrims, and tourists have been travelling there for thousands of years. This list can go on and on, and if you're someone who has visited any of these places, or others not mentioned, I'm sure you've had your own moving, profound, or perhaps mystical experience while there, whether you consider yourself religious, or not.

7. **Objects, Artifacts, & Symbols** – Throughout history, sacred objects and artifacts have been used and worn in rituals and ceremonies, and considered sacred. Many of those artifacts and objects represent a particular religion or culture, and we've come to identify them as something that expresses or symbolizes the religion to which it is

connected. For example, a cross or a crucifix is connected to Christianity and the crucifixion of Christ, and a Star of David represents Judaism. The Star of David, also known in Hebrew as the Magen David, "Shield of David," is designed with two interlocking triangles that form a six-pointed star. This is said to represent the six directions of the universe, "up, down, north, south, east, and west." This symbol appears on synagogues, Jewish tombstones, and the flag of the state of Israel. The term "Magen David" gained significance among medieval Jewish mystics, who attached magical powers to King David's shield in the same way non-Jewish magical traditions referred to the five-pointed star as the "seal of Solomon," which can be traced back to a symbol used by Arabs in the Medieval period. It is depicted as either a hexagram or a pentagram and was later adapted by Jewish Kabbalists. I'm fascinated by symbols that go back to ancient times, and the way they've been used, or changed throughout history, both positively and negatively. A pentagram, which is a five-pointed star, and used symbolically in ancient Greece and Babylonia to represent the gods and religious beliefs of their culture, has had many interpretations. The Christians believed it symbolized the five wounds of Christ. It was also used to ward off evil spirits. The Hebrews used the Pentagram as a symbol of truth, and to represent the Pentateuch, the first five books of the Hebrew Scriptures. It is said that after the death of Christ the Pentagram was the primary symbol of the Catholic Church, but after the upheaval in the Christian Church during the inquisition, which was intended to combat heresy, people who did not conform to the Church's strict views were executed, and all things associated with Paganism (which is considered a modern religion other than one of the main world religions) including the pentagram, were "deemed evil" and seen as "tools of the devil." This explains why some people today consider it an occult, or sinister, symbol. Is the symbol sinister or evil, or is it the one who is wearing or using the symbol, and for what purposes they are using it that makes it dark or evil? The same can be said of the Swastika, which in Hinduism symbolizes "surya," or "sun, prosperity, and good luck". How can we ever look at the Swastika in that way since it was inverted by Hitler, and used as the most evil symbol imaginable, associated with hatred, racism, and the genocide of six million Jewish people? What is sacred can only remain sacred if it is kept sacred by those who revere what is truly sacred.

8. **Music** – This famous quote by Shakespeare, "If music be the food of love, play on" exemplifies the beauty and power of music in our lives, and how bereft our souls would be if this "food of love" did not exist. Religious music, also called sacred music, is music originally composed or performed for religious use. There is a famous image of King David, the third King of the United Monarchy

of Israel playing the harp, or lyre, as it is also called. It is seen in the book of Psalms and is also found in Jewish and Christian scriptures. In the Hebrew Bible, David is a young shepherd who gained fame first as a musician before he became known for killing the enemy Goliath. It has been said that King David was not only an expert harpist and psalms composer who used harp therapy in the royal court of King Saul, but he was also a musicologist, and builder of classical harp designs. Although sacred music has been thought of as having its origins in religion, and dates back to medieval times, it's come a long way in its expression today. Sacred, which means "that which is set apart and special" or "not for common use" can connote that we don't bring the sacred into our daily life, especially when it comes to the type of music we listen to. For some, rock and roll ignites their soul. For someone else, rap music does it for them. Who are we to judge what fuels another's soul by the type of music they listen to, or if they feel it brings them closer to God? But, as we know, the sacred and the profane live side by side, and according to French sociologist Emile Durkheim, he considered it to be the "central characteristic of religion" and that "religion is a unified system of beliefs and practices relative to sacred things, that is to say, things set apart and forbidden." He felt that the "sacred-profane dichotomy," as his theory was called, was not equivalent to "good/evil," and if that's the case, there is a very fine line between what we might consider sacred or profane when it comes to music, especially in the 21st century. Is the sacred reserved only for something like gospel music, and music specifically meant for church and places of worship, or can that also include other types of music that I mentioned such as rap or hip-hop, which again, depending on its lyrics, some people would consider anything but sacred? One could say it's both, depending on what moves your soul. It has been said that for some listeners of rap, they've experienced spiritual ecstasy through its words, which can have religious overtones that an outsider listening might not pick up, or even understand. For me, there are different types of music that I feel moves my soul, and I too would consider these different kinds of music "food of love." This includes everything from Chopin's Nocturnes, World Music, Gregorian chants, and Canticles of Ecstasy, the music of 12th century nun, mystic, and composer Hildegard Von Bingen, which elevates my soul whenever I listen to it. And, speaking of music in the 21st century, von Bingen's chants have been set to techno rhythms, and there is a club remix of her music. Lyrics from some of my favorite songs by artists like Bob Dylan, moves my soul. I consider the lyric, "He not being born is busy dying" from Dylan's song, It's Alright Ma (I'm Only Bleeding), to be very poetic. I also consider Leonard Cohen's famous song, "Hallelujah" not only "food of love" but deeply spiritual. How many of us have moved our body, as if we too were in a trance similar to Sufi mystic Rumi in his whirling, when we listened to, or sang along with the lyric: "Hallelujah", Hallelujah, Hallelujah, Hallelujah"? That song has been adapted, re-interpreted, and sung in many churches and temples by different people of different religions, and shows you that it is the words, not just the place those words are sung, that is considered sacred by many.

In Hebrew, hallelujah means to "rejoice in praising God." Apparently, Cohen's song is about love and loss, and his biblical references are intended to provide comfort for the brokenhearted, which for many when listening to the lyrics, leads to a feeling of being taken to spiritual heights. How can we not think of music that moves our soul to be considered sacred? It calls to mind one of the most famous songs of the Beatles: "Let It Be." It has become a type of mantra for soothing our soul during "times of trouble" or in an "hour of darkness." It also mentions a holy visit, the spirit of "Mother Mary" who speaks "words of wisdom" which is an example of how what is considered divine or holy can come to us at a time of need.

Music is sacred because it comforts us, moves us, exalts us, and brings us to tears. It enters deep in our heart, and speaks to our soul, and when you're down, it can bring you right back up. When you're filled with joy, it can remind you that pain and suffering are part of life, and we must respect people who have suffered more than us, even if our life has been filled with more happy songs than sad ones. Isn't that why the Blues, which originated in the Deep South around the 1870s by African-Americans from roots in African musical tradition, can strike a chord so deep that we can feel her pain when Billie Holiday sings the lyrics in "Lady Sings the Blues"? She lets us know that she's got the blues badly and "wants the world to know just what her blues are all about." Music will always reflect the ups and downs of life, stir our emotions, and ignite our souls. And, like I talked about in the beginning of this book regarding the chemicals in our brain, research suggests that playing music, or singing together can be very potent in bringing about "social closeness through the release of endorphins." Music has also been linked to dopamine release, which regulates "mood and craving behavior." I think we would agree that music has an incredible power to bring us pleasure, and, as I said, can even lead us to spiritual heights. And if we regard this "food of love" as Shakespeare so aptly called it, as sacred, then we will experience the sacred in our listening of it, allowing music to take us to places that ignite our soul, and connects us to God, or a Divine presence that is personal to us.

I know there are many more things to add to this list of what is sacred. I feel that life without a belief in the sacred is living without reverence or awe for what moves our soul as human beings. This is why it is so very important that we connect to our spirit, as I've spoken about, and do things like take our "spiritual pulse" daily. That is having respect for ourselves, and yes, we are worthy of that respect.

Whether you believe in God or a Divine presence, or don't hold the belief that there is an "other" or a "holy other," and there is nothing beyond the "material" that exists, again, ask yourself whether there is something that holds sacred meaning for you, whatever that might be materially or spiritually. Maybe your dog is sacred to you, or your partner, or family, or children if you have any. Or, it might be a personal object, like a piece of jewelry, or heirloom that has been passed down to you, or an object of a loved one that is deceased. Maybe it's your vegetable garden that you planted with love, or the spiritual alter you took time to adorn with objects and symbols that hold sacred meaning for you.

I have no doubt there is something in your life that you hold deeply meaningful, or even sacred. Whatever that is for you, hold it dear to your heart and protect it. What lies within it, is the essence of your sacredness. You see, what is truly sacred is your soul, and when you see something, or possess something that represents sacredness, it is emanating a vibration or frequency that matches yours. You are worthy of awe and respect, and when you are in a place you feel is sacred, like a temple, church, or mosque, or travelling to a place or site that is considered holy and sacred, stop and get quiet. Go within and connect to your personal sacred place. This is your inner temple. Invite the outer sacred into your inner sacredness, and you will find that there is no separation between the sacredness that lives within you, and the sacredness that is all around us.

Let me leave you with this quote by Joseph Campbell to consider: "Your sacred space is where you can find yourself again and again."

All things are sacred
As I am sacred in all things
The sacredness I see around me
Is the sacredness that lives
Within my soul

MINDFULNESS & MYSTICISM

CHAPTER 27

MYSTICAL EXPLANATIONS OF EVIL

*We need more understanding of human nature, because the
only real danger that exists is man himself. He is the great
danger, and we are pitifully unaware of it. We know nothing
of man, far too little. His psyche should be studied, because we
are the origin of all coming evil.*

— CARL JUNG

*Mystical explanations are thought to be deep; the truth is that
they are not even shallow.*

— FRIEDRICH NIETZSCHE

The world will not be destroyed by those who do evil, but by those who watch them and do nothing.

— ALBERT EINSTEIN

An old Cherokee is teaching his grandson about life.

"A fight is going on inside me," he said to the boy.

"It is a terrible fight, and it is between two wolves.

One is evil – he is anger, envy, sorrow, regret, greed, arrogance, self-pity, guilt, resentment, inferiority, lies, false pride, superiority, and ego."

He continued, "The other is good – he is joy, peace, love, hope, serenity, humanity, kindness, benevolence, empathy, generosity, truth, compassion, and faith.

The same fight is going on inside you – and every other person, too."

The grandson thought about it for a minute and then asked his grandfather,

"Which wolf will win?"

The old Cherokee simply replied, "The one you feed."

AUTHOR UNKNOWN

When the soul is not connected to, or in communion with a divine source from which it can draw holy or sacred nourishment from, it can feel aimless, and wander away from the path of illumination. Instead, it may choose darkness from which to draw its sustenance. This is when evil can step into man's soul and redirect it towards wrongdoing and destruction. Many mystics have understood evil, and the role darkness can play in man's soul through having explored their own darkness or inner demons. For many religious mystics, they felt it was caused by the absence of God, which implies the absence of light.

When it comes to explaining evil, it's hard not to make references from the Bible, or explain it based on religion, theology, theosophy, philosophy, and something called "theodicy," which is a term coined by philosopher Gottfried Leibniz, and means "vindication of God." In other words, "justifying God's existence in light of the imperfections of the world," and evil is clearly one of those gross "imperfections." Apparently after the Holocaust, many Jewish theologians responded to the problem of evil in ways that were called "anti-theodicy" and maintained the belief that "God cannot be justified" or excused when He permits evil to happen as it did in the Holocaust. It presents the question, as Greek philosopher Epicurus put it, "Is God willing to prevent evil, but not able? Then he is not omnipotent. Is he able, but not willing? Then he is malevolent. Is he both able and willing? Then from whence comes evil?"

Many scholars, philosophers, intellectuals, and serious thinkers throughout history contemplated the existence of evil, and wrote about it extensively, yet it remains a subject that perhaps cannot be fully explained, answered, or understood. How can we possibly know better what has been defined as "profound immorality and wickedness" and has puzzled, angered, frustrated, and mystified some of the finest minds throughout the ages, and continues to do so till today?

I cannot say I have the answer for why evil exists, even though I have pondered it deeply, and probably will for the rest of my life. But what I do know is that it is something that remains one of life's most perturbing mysteries, and that is why I am choosing to approach it from a mystical perspective.

Saying that evil exists simplifies it and implies that we should just accept it as a "part of life." But, if we want to know evil better than we do, we must go towards that part of life we readily accept. Perhaps in our understanding of why we accept it, we can know not only more about the very thing we are accepting, but also why accepting something that is "profoundly immoral and wicked" is a major part of why evil continues to persist in the world.

Perhaps if we had less of a tolerance for evil, and understood that it is something to reject immediately upon recognizing it, then evil couldn't lurk as comfortably as it does, and it does lurk more comfortably than we can imagine. And wouldn't it be just as immoral and wicked for us to admit that not only do we know that evil lurks all around us, but that we also have the ability to not only accept it and consciously open our doors for evil to come into our homes, as was done by millions of Nazi sympathizers in World War II.

This collusion with evil is when the most dangerous hiding begins, and that's when evil can become less visible to us because those who choose to hide it might be harder to notice or identify, for they know how to protect evil well. Evil needs man's assistance to carry out immorality and wickedness, and that is why we must go beyond the "appearance" of what we think evil looks like, and look much deeper than what appears on the surface, which I have called "the first layer of truth." That's exactly what mysticism does. It goes beyond the layers, and the mystic lifts as many veils as possible to reach the "hidden truths" so they can understand God's "ultimate plan," which they might not know until they take their last breath. Only then, maybe, just maybe, evil can be fully understood.

Evil needs to be seen with a much finer eye, and this is the eye the mystic develops through their tireless search for the hidden truths. They know that we can no longer wait for an outward manifestation of darkness to tell us that evil has arrived, but see it way before the darkness appears, and do all that we can to shine our light upon it, which is evil's greatest enemy, our light. Remember what I said about our light in Chapter 5 - Divine thought Illumination:

"It's important to be present in the moments of our life, and by being fully awake and aware, we can not only keep our thoughts illumined, but we are cognizant of when a thought appears that is inclined to disrupt a conscious state of illumination, which happens when we shift into fear or doubt. When this occurs, we can choose to remain in divine illumination, as difficult as it may seem. You see, we have a choice to always stay in the 'light of our existence,' and that means holding thoughts in our mind that support that light."

When our mind no longer holds illumined thoughts, but instead, is taken over by fear, that's when it can be controlled, and evil can become its ruler. One of the first methods of keeping complete control over people is the use of fear, which is exactly what Hitler did so effectively to control Germany. And millions of people fell for it by allowing the darkest of darkness to sweep into their consciousness like a tsunami swallowing them in its force. If you can imagine for a moment evil looking like a giant, catastrophic wave coming in your direction, you would know in a split second that it is unstoppable, and your fate has been determined right then and there by those who have chosen not to be in "union with a transcendent reality" but with a reality that is in union with evil.

Evil is very clever at looking for its finest hosts, and it needn't look too far to find them. How shocking it was to know how many hosts there were in Germany who were not only ready to invite evil into themselves, but to execute it in the most heinous, and incomprehensible ways. It will forever be mind-boggling, at the amount of evil man was capable of carrying out during that darkest time in history. But we must, as I said, not put our focus on knowing that evil exists, which it does, and probably always will, but more on how we are the executors of evil. Without us, evil could never do all that it does, has done, and will continue to do unless we, as I said, "stay in the light of our existence, and hold thoughts in our mind that support that light."

We mustn't take lightly the importance of keeping our minds illumined, and this is a daily practice with the use of Mindfulness. It's incumbent upon us to be present in all of the moments of our life, and aware of not only the darkness that lurks outside of us, but, most importantly, the darkness that lurks within.

Psychologist Carl Jung, who wrote a great deal on evil, felt that if man's shadow, the darker aspects of his psyche remains unconscious, "it will wreak havoc in his life, and darkness will manifest out in the world." He also said about the shadow: "Unfortunately, there can be no doubt that man is, on the whole, less good than he imagines himself or wants to be. Everyone carries a shadow, and the less it is embodied in the individual's conscious life, the blacker and denser it is. At all counts, it forms an unconscious snag, thwarting our most well-meant intentions."

This lets us know how important it is to be conscious and aware of those darker aspects of ourselves of which we may not be so proud. Unless we shine a light on the darkness that lives inside our own soul, it will, as Jung also said, "take possession of our being, exerting control of our thoughts." Man will always struggle to keep his mind "illumined" because, as the Cherokee elder says to his grandson in the story above, "The same fight is going on inside you and every other person too." And, when the boy asks his grandfather, "Which wolf will win?" the old Cherokee simply replied, "The one you feed."

Keeping our minds illumined with thoughts of light and love is our only hope for keeping evil at bay. It waits, lurking all around us. Evil, as a force, wants nothing more than for a single deceptive or misleading thought to take us down the wrong path and lead us to the door of darkness, where we feel we must enter. And this is the very moment when we abandon ourselves. We not only lose the fight of the two conflicting wolves within us, but accept the evil wolf consuming the good one, and off we go looking to prey on those whose good wolf has won the fight within them.

Perhaps that's what we are: a two-sided wolf, one good, one evil, and we walk this earth either winning or losing the battle of light versus dark within us. And, if we know this about ourselves, that there will always be a moral struggle we grapple with, then we can stop asking questions like, "Who is responsible for evil?" or "Where does evil come from?" or "Why does evil exist?" Instead, we can look no further than our own shadow, and be unafraid to examine it closely, cutting away those thoughts that are dark or evil, like a cancer that wants to eat away at our soul.

Be your own gatekeeper, and save yourself from the darkness; the evil wolf that wants to win the fight inside you. And the way to do this, as I said, is to keep your mind illumined, which is a mind of spiritual light.

In spite of knowing that evil exists, never give up hope that it can be defeated. This beautiful quote by Vincent Van Gogh speaks of having hope:

"Many people seem to think it foolish, even superstitious, to believe that the world could still change for the better. And it is true that in winter it is sometimes so bitingly cold that one is tempted to say, 'What do I care if there is a summer; its warmth is no help to me now.' Yes, evil often seems to surpass good. But then, in spite of us, and without our permission, there comes at last an end to the bitter frosts. One morning the wind turns, and there is a thaw. And so, I must still have hope."

Yes, we must have hope. Each, and every one of us.

Darkness lurks

Like a phantom that wishes to inhale

My very soul

I am the light

It seeks to extinguish

I am the light

It can never

Destroy

MINDFULNESS & MYSTICISM

CHAPTER 28

THE LIGHT
OF MYSTICISM

People will do anything, no matter how absurd, in order to avoid facing their own souls. One does not become enlightened by imagining figures of light, but by making the darkness conscious.

— CARL JUNG

If the light is in your heart, you will find your way home.

— RUMI

We can easily forgive a child who is afraid of the dark; the real tragedy of life is when men are afraid of the light.

— PLATO

There is a crack in everything. That's how the light gets in.

— LEONARD COHEN

Let us go even further now, and explore the conflict between good and evil, which has been written about, as I said, by some of the greatest thinkers throughout history, such as Nieitzsche's, Beyond Good and Evil; Jung's, On Evil; Thomas Aquinas, On Evil; and Theodicy: Essays on the Goodness of God, the Freedom of Man and the Origin of Evil by Wilhelm Leibniz von Gottfried, to name a few. This is a struggle that is well known about man's psychological turmoil, so it's fair to say that perhaps nothing revelatory has been realized about good vs. evil, other than we know that this conflict is alive and real, and will continue to exist as part of what plagues the human condition.

What needs to be looked at more closely, and mysticism likes to look at things more closely, is what progress have we made in learning about the dark side of our personality, or what Jung called the "shadow" and how have we brightened our light to triumph over it?

If we look at mysticism as the union with the Absolute, the Infinite, God, or whatever holds sacred meaning for us, then we understand that this "union" is one of man merging with his higher self through an expansion of awareness. The true nature of our being is what triumphs over the dark aspects of our personality so that a state of "wholeness" or "oneness" can be realized.

We become illumined by our merging with the light, or what I would like to call the source of creation; that which we come from, and that to which we will return.

This light, in my opinion, is the personification of mysticism because in its radiance all things are transformed, and this is when we can, as Jung said, "make the darkness conscious."

A mystical experience is when we glimpse, or experience this radiance of divine light. When people are fortunate enough to feel something like "exalted and indescribable beauty," as Evelyn Underhill did "walking down a squalid street," that is when "the light gets in," as Leonard Cohen says in his quote. Perhaps "there is a crack in everything," as Cohen believed, and if we recognize that the light will always find its way in, then we will look for ways to help it enter. That's how darkness, or evil, is transformed.

We must think of ourselves as transformers of darkness and not wait until evil shows up at our door, as I spoke about in the previous chapter - Mystical Explanations of Evil. And, if it does, it may come disguised as something other than what it truly is, which is the power evil has. It can appear in many different forms, and if you are not good at identifying darkness for what it is, "a lack of illumination" then know it has come for your light, and will suck it from you so fast like a vampire, you will not even know that your light has been taken from you.

Walking the mystical path means that you are able to see darkness and evil extremely well because you are in union with divine light, and this is your natural state of being. And, if, or when evil pays you a visit, because evil likes to do that occasionally to test our level of awareness, you can dispel it with your light, which is a type of light that is illumined by a higher state of consciousness.

Remember what I said about consciousness in Chapter 12 - States of Consciousness: "There are many states, meaning levels of awareness our consciousness can be functioning on, and depending on how awake, present, and aware we are of ourselves, others, and our environment, determines our state of consciousness."

So, what level of consciousness do you think you are functioning on?

To refresh your memory, these levels include the following:

1. Waking consciousness – The state of consciousness you experience when you are awake and aware of your thoughts, feelings, and perceptions.
2. Sleep consciousness – The state of waking consciousness paused or turned off when not dreaming.
3. Dreaming consciousness – The transition into a dream state from waking consciousness.
4. Transcendental consciousness – The state of consciousness after waking, sleeping, and dreaming states. It is described as "wakeful, alert, and conscious of self."
5. Cosmic consciousness – The state of a higher form

of consciousness than that possessed by the
ordinary man.

6. God consciousness – The consciousness of a
   higher self, transcendental reality, or God.
7. Unity consciousness – The state of consciousness
   that unites us to ourselves, others, nature, or the
   God of our understanding.

I also pointed out previously that "the first three levels
of consciousness are experienced by every human being
with a functioning nervous system." The last four levels
are thought to become accessible only as one meditates on
a regular basis, according to a theory based on the practice
of Transcendental Meditation, which is a technique derived from the ancient Vedic tradition of India by Maharishi Mahesh Yogi for "avoiding distracting thoughts and
promoting a state of relaxed awareness." But, not everyone
is a meditator, and you can experience those other, or
higher states of consciousness by being in a state of "relaxed awareness," which Mindfulness helps you realize.

When we are in a state of present moment awareness,
we are much more likely to encounter the divine light
that is around us at every given moment. Yes, darkness
and evil are lurking right beside it, but when we are "at
one with the light," and in a more heightened state of
awareness, which raises our consciousness, we are in a
state of illumination. This is when the "light of mysticism"
accompanies you on your life journey, like a protective

shield that deflects darkness rather than attracts or ab-
sorbs it. Think of this protective shield as possessing
magical powers the way King David's shield protected
him. If you believe that you have this protection around
you, as well as God's protection, which the Bible says
King David had, then you will feel confident that darkness cannot penetrate you, for you are impenetrable to it.

But know that you needn't go in search of the light of
mysticism because if you are aligned with it, it is radiating
from your being already. You are the light. There is no separation between you and divine radiance. You and divine
presence are one. There is no longer a disconnection,
detachment, or uncoupling between your divine light,
and the "refulgence," the radiant, gleaming light of this
"source of creation" of which I spoke. It is pure, luminous
energy that we can tap into and connect with always. It is
our sense of separation, which is an illusion, that keeps us
stuck in lower, or more base levels of consciousness.

And until we take a deeper look at the inner shadow,
we will keep thinking and believing that the darkness exists only outside of ourselves. No, it is the darkness within
that is the most dangerous darkness there is, which is why
we must shine a light on our inner darkness first before
we can dispel, overcome, or defeat darkness without.

Let me guide you to visit your darkness with this
meditation, and by letting the light "enter it," you can
allow for transformation to take place, and overcome the
darkness with your light.

1. Find a quiet place to sit.

2. You can either close your eyes, or keep them open if you wish.

3. Take a few deep breaths in and out.

4. Note what feeling(s), or any sensation(s) you are experiencing in your body, and simply observe them.

5. Imagine a white, protective light around you.

6. Imagine this white, protective light around you now permeating your entire being, from the soles of your feet to the crown of your head.

7. See yourself glowing with this white, protective light, which is your auric field, energetic layers that always surround you.

8. Visualize yourself enter into the depths of your being.

9. Think of it as the secret room of your soul.

10. See yourself open a door and enter a room of darkness.

11. Again, note what feeling(s) or sensation(s) you are experiencing in your body, and simply observe them.

12. If you feel something like fear, or anxiety, and wish to stop, give yourself permission to do so.

13. If you'd like to continue, tell yourself, "I can overcome darkness."

14. Ask your darkness to reveal itself to you.

15. It might come to you in the form of a thought,

an image, or external voice.

16. What do you see or hear?
17. Say silently, "I am here to shine my light on you."
18. Say silently, "I am more powerful than you."
19. Say silently, "You are the absence of light."
20. Say silently, "My divine light has entered you."
21. Say silently, "I have transformed you with my light."
22. See the white light that is emanating from your being, light up the entire room.
23. Say silently, "This room of darkness is forever transformed by my light."
24. See yourself walk out of this room, and close the door behind you.
25. When you are ready, open your eyes if they are closed, and transition out of this meditation.
26. Take the time you need to be with what you have experienced in this transformational meditation.

What this meditation does is make your own darkness "conscious to you," which is what Jung felt we needed to do in order to both understand it, and transform it. And, this meditation can be done whenever you want to process your darkness, or "shadow," as Jung called it.

The "Mysticism of Light" is a path for you to walk daily. It is your sovereign right to walk the path of divine light because that is the path you were born to take. As Rumi says in his quote above, "If the light is in your heart, you will find your way home."

The Light of Mysticism
Shines on me
As I walk the path
Of awakening
When I encounter darkness
I am protected and shielded
By the light

MINDFULNESS & MYSTICISM

CHAPTER 29

THE WAY OF
THE LIGHTWORKER

If you light a lamp for someone else,
It will also brighten your path.

— BUDDHA

Remember the clear light, the pure clear white light from
which everything in the universe comes,

To which everything in the universe returns, the original
nature of your own mind.

The natural state of the universe unmanifest.

Let go into the clear light, trust it, merge with it.

It is your own true nature. It is home.

— TIBETAN BOOK OF THE DEAD

There is a light that shines beyond all things on earth,
Beyond the highest, the very highest heavens.
This is the light that shines in your heart.

— CHANDOGYA UPANISHAD

A definition of a "Lightworker" is someone who has the ability to sense or intuit what people are thinking, feeling, or need, and helps raise the consciousness of others.

I would say that if we practice Mindfulness, we are naturally more aware of the needs of others, and therefore can function as a Lightworker, whether we intend to or not. In Chapter 24 - Supernatural Powers, I talk about how we have "innate, natural powers that can be considered supernatural, paranormal, transcendent, metaphysical, or even other worldly." I also said that we have the ability to transcend our "humanness," and be guided more by our spirit, which keeps us connected to the supernatural or transcendent. I believe we are evolving in our consciousness at a rapid speed, and that each of us, if we are committed to the path of awakening, meaning we are choosing to keep our thoughts "illumined" for the purpose of heightening our awareness and raising our consciousness can live in a more transcendent state. Being a "Lightworker" is one of those heightened states to be in.

If we "remember the clear light, the pure clear white light from which everything in the universe comes, to which everything in the universe returns," as the quote above from the Tibetan Book of the Dead says (a text that is recited "to ease the consciousness of a recently deceased person through death, and assist them into a favorable rebirth"), then we know that this "clear, pure light" is the "original nature of our own mind." Not only the nature of our own mind, but "the natural state of the universe," as the quote also says.

Being a Lightworker isn't something only other people can be, which can also be said for those who are healers. Yes, there are people who are trained in the areas of healing, like physicians, therapists, and shamans, and their work is devoted to helping others get well, or heal. But, that doesn't mean that the light needed to shine on someone who is distressed, ailing, or sick, can't be the light that comes from our own hearts. If we shined that light on ourselves when we are feeling depressed or anxious, or outward towards others with something like a smile, a hug, or uttering the words, "I love you" more often, wellness would be our natural state, which it is, when we don't disrupt it. We would stand a much greater chance of not waiting for our hearts and souls to be lonely or starved, which is why we reach for things like drugs and alcohol, or anything that stops us from feeling our pain. If we move towards the light, and bask in the warmth of what can nourish us rather than hurt or harm us, we too can function as a Lightworker.

We would "let go into the clear light, trust it, merge with it," as the Tibetan Book of the Dead quote also says. Again, "it is your own true nature," and more poignantly, as the quote ends, "it is home." We are walking towards this sacred "home," if we believe that the union that we seek in our souls is that of the mystical. This is the home I believe we are searching for, which I also called, "the source of creation," that which we come from, and that to which we will return. We just need to help one another get there, and we can, if we consciously guide ourselves there with every step.

But we will have days when that will be difficult because our hearts will be heavy, and we won't feel that our thoughts are illumined. What can we do when we don't feel that we are the Lightworker of our own heart or soul, and are struggling to walk our way home again? How can we stay on the mystical path so that we remain in union with that which is sacred?

We must make a concerted effort to connect to the light within, even if we feel it isn't there. It is always there, but the dense energy of negativity, fear, or the worries of everyday life can easily seep into our minds. If we aren't careful, or fully present, that energy permeates our light, and that is when darkness, or even evil, is waiting to steal our light.

Darkness works like that. It is a thief that is lurking closely, and if we know this about darkness, we make certain that our light is always turned up way high, even when we may feel emotionally low. You see, our inner light is always there, as I said, but if we believe that it isn't, that is when we succumb, or even surrender, to darkness because we are convinced that we are too weak to fight it. This is when one can slip into depression, and thoughts of suicide can come as a solution to rescue us from our pain and suffering. No. Suicide is not a solution for our pain and suffering. Suicide is a brutal act of murder. It is killing yourself on purpose. It is dying at your own hand. It is darkness winning, and you mustn't let it win. Fight for your life because it is worth fighting for more than anything else you can fight for.

These dark thoughts that take possession of you are beliefs, my friend, and nothing but thoughts that we tell ourselves, convincing us they are true when they are not. What I suggest is that even when you are feeling down or low, imagine your inner light flickering like a well-lit fire coming from a fireplace in a beautiful sanctuary of safety and comfort. This is your refuge, your shelter from the darkness whenever you feel that it is beckoning you to come towards it. You are a Lightworker, are you not? You are not willing to give your light away, are you? And if you are, please ask yourself why.

Remember, your light is lit from within, and if you need assistance keeping it lit, and you feel you cannot do this for yourself, ask for help. Ask a holy presence to aid you. If you're religious, ask for help from God, or a God of your choosing. If you are not religious, and do not believe in a God, ask the invisible to make itself visible to you. It will. This is mysticism aiding you. It is there even if you cannot see it. I mentioned in Chapter 16 - The Human Spirit, in Jewish mysticism, there is something called "Chokhmah"; this is the all-encompassing Supernal

Wisdom that vitalizes all of creation. There will be times when you will need to connect to your supernal wisdom, which means a type of wisdom that is defined as coming from "on high" or the "heavens."

Can you see how much help there is for you? If ever, for one moment, you fall into the trap of illusion, and do not believe that you are surrounded by divine light, you must stop and dig deep within your soul and ask for help. You are a Lightworker! Yes, you are. And now, you must learn how to make your light work for you at all times. This is the initiation needed for the mystic, to learn how to wield the infinite power of the light. You can ask to learn this if you'd like. Would you like to learn how to use this power?

Let us begin with a meditation to keep you in Light worker mode:

1. Sit somewhere quiet.
2. Close your eyes.
3. Take a few deep breaths in and out.
4. See yourself surrounded and protected by white, radiant light as I had you do in Chapter 28 - The Light of Mysticism. Remember, this is your auric field, the energetic layers that always surround you.
5. Once this vision is clear and strong for you, say silently to yourself, "I am a Lightworker."
6. Say silently, "I walk the path of a Lightworker."
7. Say silently, "I have the power as a Lightworker to shine my light wherever I am, and on whoever I choose to."
8. Say silently, "My role as a Lightworker is important."
9. Say silently, "My intention as a Lightworker is to raise consciousness in others."
10. Say silently, "When I doubt my role or intention as a Lightworker, my mind needs to be restored with illumined thoughts."
11. Say silently, "The illumined mind is the mind of a Lightworker."
12. Say silently, "I am a Lightworker."
13. Say silently, "My mind is illumined."
14. When you are ready, open your eyes and transition out of this meditation.

A Lightworker knows that they are here on this planet to help wake people up and connect them with their true, divine spirit, so that they can be in a mystical union, which I've been speaking about. This sacred union is the relationship between your soul and God, or whatever the Divine is for you. This relationship is like a consummation of divine love, and it can only be realized in an awakened state of consciousness, first and foremost.

The role of the Lightworker is an extremely important one. We are living in a time when consciousness raising should be considered an urgent necessity, a call to action, meaning that we no longer have time to waste, not even a single moment. We are facing extremely serious threats to the human species, and according to the Cambridge Project at Cambridge University, which is dedicated to the "study and mitigation of risks that could lead to human extinction or civilization collapse," the greatest threats to the human species are "man-made," and they list them as follows: "Global warming, AI (Artificial Intelligence), which I mentioned earlier, nuclear war, and rogue biotechnology," which is used for genetic engineering. What this tells us in bright neon lights is that we need to roll up our sleeves and get our virtual lightsabers out big time.

It is time for us to think of ourselves as the Jedi Knights in the Star Wars movies, and know that the fight between light and dark, or good vs. evil, exists. Which side we choose to align ourselves with depends on the

inner work we do with our own shadow, as Jung empha-
sized the importance of. How well we navigate our own
internal fight between the good wolf vs. the evil one is
which one we feed, and that will be the one that "wins," as
the old Cherokee teaching goes. It also defines the good
wolf as embodying "joy, peace, love, hope, serenity, humanity, kindness, benevolence, empathy, generosity, truth,
compassion, and faith." The evil wolf embodies "anger,
envy, sorrow, regret, greed, arrogance, self-pity, guilt, resentment, inferiority, lies, false pride, superiority, and ego."

So, ask yourself which wolf you are feeding, and
whether you are in genuine Lightworker mode. Do you
want to be? Each of us must ask ourselves, "Why am
I here?" and "How awake and conscious am I?" Most
importantly, "How am I using my light?" If you don't
know, or choose not to know, but instead think you're
here to be negative, complain, lament, or begrudge the life
you feel you've been given, then you are sucking energy
from the planet rather than helping to replenish it. And
that's the crisis we are witnessing today. This is a planet of
approximately 7.7 billion people, and how many of them
would you guess are Lightworkers vs. people who are
free-loaders or energy vampires? My guess is that there
are far more people who are taking from this earth rather
than giving or putting back something that is positive
or helpful, and we wonder why we are faced with what
seems like insurmountable problems, not to mention an

increase in violence, hate, and racism, which fuels the path of destruction on this planet.

This is because so many people do not keep their minds illumined, nor do they function from a selfless, compassionate place in their hearts, which emanates light. Each of us is a Lightworker, if we want to be. But, if you believe that only other people function in this capacity, then you are accepting this about yourself, and choosing perhaps to live more of an "ordinary life," which I spoke about in Chapter 4 - Transcending the Ordinary. If you subscribe to this quote by Augustus that "Everyone wants to lead an extraordinary life," then perhaps you are someone who feels you are entitled to one, and you most certainly are. You can be, if you see this life as an opportunity to transcend the ordinary, and live as an extraordinary Lightworker. Let the light that shines in your heart lead the way, and consciousness will rise, both individually and collectively.

"Non Ducor Duco"

"I am not led, I lead."

I am a Lightworker

My light guides me

And shines a light on others

May we light up the world

With the light in our hearts

And awaken together

In Divine wisdom

MINDFULNESS & MYSTICISM

CHAPTER 30

NONDUALISM

Wisdom tells me I am nothing, love tells me I am everything.
Between the two, my life flows.

— SRI NISARGADATTA MAHARAJ

You and I are all as much continuous with
the physical universe as a wave is continuous
with the ocean.

— ALAN WATTS

Relationships only work in a spiritual sense when you
and I really see that we are one.

— RAM DASS

Quantum physics thus reveals a basic oneness
of the universe.

— ERWIN SCHRODINGER

I have spoken extensively on mysticism as being "in union with a transcendent reality," and whether that's in union with God, or whatever a Divine source or presence means to you, it essentially means that you are not separated from this higher reality, or a transcendent state of consciousness.

As I talked about in Chapter 13 - Higher Consciousness, "When we are in a higher state of consciousness, we are more open to having a mystical experience. And, when we practice Mindfulness, and are in present moment awareness, we are able to raise our awareness to such levels that we can feel as if our consciousness is like an ever-flowing stream in our awakening. So, in essence, I'm saying that all of this is the perfect recipe for our consciousness to reign supreme. However, nothing can get heightened if we, ourselves, are not in an active state of awareness."

I hope by now you are practicing Mindfulness and keeping yourself in "present moment awareness" as much as possible. This must become a daily practice, and if, or when, you find yourself about to slip out of a moment, you gently bring yourself back to the moment you are in by doing something as simple as focusing on your breath.

A very easy breathing exercise to help bring you into present moment awareness, and one of my personal favorites is this:

1. Take a breath in and count: 1...2...3...4...1
2. Release your breath and count: 1...2...3...4...2
3. Take another breath in and count:
   1...2...3...4...3
4. Release another breath out, and count:
   1...2...3...4...4

Get into the habit of doing this whenever your mind begins to wander, and once you get really good at bringing yourself right back into the present moment, focusing on a single breath will suffice, and you will no longer need to count. Falling into the traps of distraction are far too easy to take you out of the moment you are in, and this, unfortunately, takes you off the mystical path. Remember what I said about the mystical path. It is a great privilege to be on it, and mystical experiences don't just happen to us because we insist that they should. By staying present and fully aware in a moment, you are open to a mystical experience, or available for what I call "Visits of Ecstasy," the title of Chapter 20. You need to, as I said in that chapter, "Stay present, and understand you are not separate from God, or a Divine presence, but "at one" with all that exists." This brings us to "Nondualism," also called non-duality that I touched upon earlier. I will go more in depth here.

In spirituality, this means "not two," and having an awareness that is "without dichotomies." But the definition I find most telling is having a "mature state of consciousness," and as we know about the different states of consciousness we can achieve, as I talked about in Chapter 12 - States Of Consciousness, "There are many states, meaning levels of awareness our consciousness can be functioning on, and depending on how awake, present, and aware we are of ourselves, others, and our environment; determines our state of consciousness."

A "mature state of consciousness" is what's needed to live in a nondual state because it requires serious preparation to be in it. Like living the mystical life, it's serious business, meaning you need to be someone who takes your level of consciousness very seriously. Aspire to raise it so that you can reach the higher levels of awareness that are necessary to raise not only your consciousness but also helps raise the all-pervasive energy on the planet. Whether you consider yourself a Lightworker, or not, we are all beings of light, and if we keep our thoughts illumined, which raises the vibration and frequency of our light, we are doing the work I believe we are meant to do on this planet.

We no longer must think that it is others, like religious or mythical figures, who can do the work for us. Believing in the "coming of the Messiah" is waiting for a savior or a liberator to come and anoint us with the holy oil that redeems us somehow. As you know by now, this is not a book on religion, even though I make some religious references. And if you do believe in the Messiah, I do not wish to disrespect your beliefs by inferring that a Messiah is not coming. I have no way of knowing who, or what will come to anoint us, redeem us, resurrect us, lead us, or save us. If there is such a being coming, I hope we'll be ready to receive them by making sure that our own inner temple is beautiful and whole, and that we can invite them in to see how well we've kept our inner sanctum filled with light and love. I don't know about you, but if a holy being is on their way to us, I'd like to make them proud of how hard I've worked to show that I am worthy of such a visit.

It's definitely time to realize a "mature state of consciousness," as far as I'm concerned, and one of the ways to do this is to stop being wish-washy in our commitment to heightening our awareness, and raising consciousness, both individually and collectively. The Buddha said, "Above all, don't wobble," and what I take this to mean is to be in harmony with the undivided mind. Yes, there will be times that we may feel uncertain, or divided, and is it possible to "live without dichotomies" all of the time? No, it isn't, especially since life is full of dichotomies and contradictions. But Mindfulness, which is not only an excellent practice for helping us stay present and makes us more aware of life's ups and down, dichotomies, contradictions, and the unexpected changes and vicissitudes we will invariably experience on this life journey.

What Mindfulness does is it helps us maintain equanimity in the face of change and accept it maturely without reacting. This is the type of "mature consciousness" we want to be in so we can be aware of when we slip into duality. We can prepare ourselves to resist thoughts that try and pull us in the direction of doubt or fear, which leads us to believe we are not enough or whole. We may not be fully enlightened the way the Buddha became, but we have the seed of enlightenment in us, which makes us Buddha beings in the making. It is our negative and fear-based thoughts that keep us in a state of dualism, which creates illusion and delusion. Instead of glimpsing the seed of enlightenment, which illumined thoughts can help us see, we slip into dualism, and lose sight of the seed of enlightenment within. This is how forgetting happens. We forget who we are, and it is the path of awakening, and our commitment to nondualism, that helps us remember. But it takes much practice and work, and you're either up for it, or you're not.

Meditation is a wonderful practice to observe the duality of the mind. By sitting with non-judgment, you can witness your dualistic thoughts, which can stem from what is also called the "egoic mind" the negative self-talk, chatter, and "everything outside of pure consciousness that wants to sabotage your inner peace." This is what I like to call our "inner knowing." The egoic mind, and all of its nonsense, wants to do nothing more than to pull us out of the moment of contentment or bliss, and we allow for it again and again. As I said early on in this book, maybe we just can't handle feeling a natural high or bliss all the time, so we sabotage it whenever the possibility of it comes too close. We think instead that the only way we can experience bliss or euphoria is by taking some type of drug, or drinking alcohol excessively. We have yet to know the pure brilliance that we are, and hopefully on this mystical path of awakening, you will come to know who you truly are if you're willing to get out of your own way long enough. This is my intention for you. This journey began when you embraced the mystical journey and said to yourself that you are ready to take it. Hopefully, if you have, you know and accept that the work doesn't stop once this book is over. You must continue the journey of awakening each and every day. Remember what I said about "mature consciousness." It takes practice, and things like Mindfulness, meditation, contemplation, and doing all of the exercises and meditations I've shared with you up till now.

The path of the mystic is an extraordinary one, but it can also be hard, difficult, demanding, and, at times, both mind boggling and mind bending. Yes, it can shake you right out of your comfort zone, and just when you think you've mastered the "monkey mind," which I mentioned, and is a Buddhist term for the "restless, confused, inconsistent, indecisive," and overall trouble making mind, you realize you haven't. Let that be humbling, not frustrating. I view this as part of the mystical journey. Remember, you are lifting the veils of illusion, one by one, and if sometimes you think you've lifted them all, guess what? That's your ego mind talking! Keep lifting those veils because there will be many more along the path of awakening. Focus on being a good "veil lifter" and you will lift them faster and faster. Don't worry, you will get respites along the way. But to awaken means you cannot afford to be asleep at the wheel. As I said, that's what naps are for.

Try, if you can, to meditate, or give yourself time in the day to sit quietly, allowing yourself to be aware of your thoughts and cognizant of the activity of your mind. Does your mind seem restless? Are you experiencing dualistic thoughts? If so, what are your thoughts telling you? To be more, do more, have more? To be there, but not here? To be who you're not, and live inauthentically? To feel ordinary and undeserving of a more extraordinary life? These are the types of thoughts that take us away from truth; the truth that we are perfect, and by this, I mean spiritual perfection. This type of perfection means that we are exquisite beings who are at one with all that exists on this earth plane and the cosmos, and there is no separation or dualism, other than what exists in our own minds, which tells us we are not the light that fills our souls, and made of "star stuff," as Carl Sagan said. We are also "a way for the universe to know itself," as Sagan also said, which means we must continue to awaken, and remember who we are as we find our way back home to where we came from, and this life journey is taking us there. But we must be present to see the signposts along the way, or we will get lost, which is why we must stay present, aware, and conscious.

Let me guide you in a third eye meditation to help you stay present, and be in a non-dual state to connect to a deeper knowing of who you are. This meditation can release a natural chemical in the brain known as DMT, (N-Dimethyltryptamine), which has been called the "spirit molecule." Like the drug that creates a psychedelic experience, it's believed by "pseudo-scientists" (I guess these "assertions" or "beliefs" do not "satisfy the requirements and practices of true science," as pseudoscience is defined) that DMT exists in the pineal gland, also referred to as the "third eye" or "inner eye," and where this molecule is produced. We can experience this psychedelic, or transcendent feeling when we dream, and supposedly during birth and death.

My goal is for this book to help you access these natural chemicals in your brain so you can experience more transcendent states of consciousness. Hopefully, one day these practices and beliefs will be acceptable, even commonplace, and we shall become more powerful than the chemists and pharmacists upon whom we are so dependent. We will live as alchemists. This is how we functioned in ancient times. An alchemist was considered a type of chemist, and also called a "wizard" because those who were competent, capable, and true alchemists could not only turn metal into gold (which I believe is a metaphor for transforming our "baser" or "animal tendencies" into an "illuminated" or spiritual being in a modern alchemy context), but an alchemist could also make special elixirs that could cure people. Imagine that! We can cure people, which means we can cure ourselves. Unfortunately, our "dualistic thinking" tells us otherwise, and we forget who we are, and what we are capable of, unless, of course, we choose to remember. Do you wish to remember?

Let us begin:

1. Find a quiet place to sit.
2. Close your eyes.
3. Take a few deep breaths in and out.
4. With your eyes closed, roll your eyes slightly upward and focus on the space between your eyes; the "third eye" or "inner eye." Consider this a place where you can see into the cosmic truth of your existence, and the universe.
5. You may notice an orb of light there. The more you keep your two eyes focused on it, the more this orb of light might appear to be growing in size as if now you have entered into the orb rather than just observing it. It might change in color from white to a rainbow of colors and pulsate or undulate in its vibration. Or it

might be complete stillness, with no color or motion.
Whatever it looks like, allow yourself to feel the energy, or warmth of it, if it feels like a bodily sensation. If
you feel that this orb of light is taking you deeper and
deeper into it, allow yourself to go there. Do not fear
going deeper, but if at any time you feel that you are
not ready to be taken deeper into this radiant light,
know that you can stop this meditation at any time.
If you have thoughts of fear, acknowledge them, and
try to observe them, as if they are like clouds moving
across the sky therefore impermanent. Or, ask yourself silently, "Do I wish to continue?" If the answer is
"no," then stop the meditation, and accept that you do
not wish to do this at this time. Hopefully you will
try again when you are ready. If you answered "yes,"
continue on.

6. Say silently, "I have entered into the radiant light
   of my being."
7. Say silently, "This is the radiant light of the universe."
8. Say silently, "I am at one with the radiant light of
   the universe."
9. Say silently, "The universe and I are one."
10. Say silently, "There is no end to this radiant light."
11. Say silently, "This radiant light fills my being at all
    times."
12. Say silently, "This radiant light has no duality."
13. You might feel as if you are floating in a vast,
    never-ending space of the universe. Allow your-

self to float for as long as you wish to. Feel the lightness of your being, as if it is suspended in a space of no time or thought.

14. Feel your "small self" disappear which means the "who" or "what" we think we are, and experience what can be called "oneness," or "unity consciousness." This is the state we can feel in meditation, or when having a mystical experience. Far too often it is fleeting, but now you have an opportunity to extend it because you are consciously aware that you are in a state of "oneness," not separate from anything, which can also be called the "oceanic feeling," a phrase coined by French mystic, Romain Rolland, that refers to "a sensation of eternity." This awareness of oneness is like having a lucid dream where you are fully aware of being in a dream, and can direct it to where you want it to go. The same can be said of this meditation. You are directing it exactly where you want it to go, and the deeper you allow yourself to free fall into it, the more extraordinary it will be. You might feel yourself disappear entirely, which is a state of "no-self" when we let go of our identity or persona. This can feel as if you're disappearing. Again, if you feel fear, you can stop at any time, but remember, you are the creator of this meditation, just like you create your dreams.

15. If you find yourself disappearing into the radiant void of light, imagine this light as pure energy, which you are.

16. Say silently, "This light is what brought me here in birth form."

17. Say silently, "This light is where I will return when my spirit leaves my body."

18. I know what a dreamy state this is to be in, and time can truly stand still in this meditation, but we must return back to the body. So, when you are ready, slowly open your eyes.

19. Take time to ground yourself, and feel yourself root back in the earth. If you want more grounding, go outside barefoot and feel the earth under your feet, or stand under a tree, or wrap your arms around it.

20. This meditation will serve you best if you don't abruptly transition into another activity. Ideally, it would be a good meditation to do followed by a hot cup of tea, or a bath.

I hope you experienced non-duality in this meditation. Even if you had thoughts of fear or doubt come up, I hope you were able to observe them and recognized their impermanence. If we looked at our negative or disruptive thoughts as we would a fly or gnat that is moving around us, we would know that something that "small," as annoying as it can be, can be gone in a second, and we needn't give it more energy than necessary. We can waste a tremendous amount of good energy on what I like to call "useless thoughts," which constantly derails us from much more interesting, important, productive, or even fascinating things we can focus on, experience, or choose to spend time on.

The goal is to stay in a state of "Luminous Mind," which I mentioned earlier. This is a Buddhist term that means a "mind of clear light" or a "brightly shining mind." We don't want to just experience this when we're in meditation. Yes, a meditation like the one you just did will put you in a state of luminous mind for sure if you allow yourself to go there. But the ultimate goal is to be in a "mind of clear light" not just in mediation, but in as many moments as we can. Mindfulness is our greatest guide for this because it helps us stay present, and the more present we are, the more we can clear our mind of any thoughts that do not serve our wellbeing. We want to keep it filled with illumined thoughts that tell us we are not separate from anything or anyone. This is a natural state to be in, and it is unnatural to think we are separate from the oneness we have felt whenever we have been lucky enough to experience it.

This book is a road map for you to have a luminous mind so that you can be ready for mystical experiences, and when they visit you, you know that this is exactly where you are supposed to be. There will be no doubt in your mind because doubt of the numinous is not an option for a mystic. They know that they are in union with something that is so divine, to doubt it, or "look upon it as wrong," as Evelyn Underhill said, would be "an unthinkable absurdity."

I disappeared

And I realized

I am at one with

Everything that exists

So therefore

I too exist as something

Much greater than

The small self

I am a spark of the

Divine

Which is all

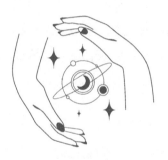

MINDFULNESS & MYSTICISM

CHAPTER 31

SPIRITUAL INITIATION

*We take spiritual initiation when we become conscious of the
Divine within us, and thereby contact the Divine without us.*

— DION FORTUNE

*The only initiation which I advocate and which I look for
with all the ardor of my soul, is that by which we are able
to enter in the Heart of God within us, and there make an
Indissoluble Marriage, which makes us the Friend and Spouse
of the Repairer....there is no other way to arrive at this Holy
Initiation than for us to delve more and more into the depth of
our Soul and to not let go of the prize until we have succeeded
in liberating its lively and vivifying origin.*

— LOUIS CLAUDE DE SAINT-MARTIN

If the mystic is someone who attains union with God, the absolute, or a type of reality that is considered transcendent, sacred, or even holy, it doesn't mean they have a need to talk about it or share it with others. Some people who walk the path of the mystical, or have had mystical experiences, might choose to keep it private. For them, this sacred path remains hidden in the depths of their being, and that's where it will stay.

If you consider yourself a mystic, or would like to walk the mystical path, you can choose to be private about it or share it with whomever you wish to. I feel tremendously grateful that I was able to find the works of some of the incredible mystics throughout the ages who shared their mystical experiences and wisdom with us, those who chose the mystical path as a way of life. People like Evelyn Underhill, Gurdjieff, Hildegard von Bingen, Rumi, Plotinus, Pythagoras, and Thomas Merton.

Although he preferred to be seen as a "man of science," I view Carl Jung as one of the great mystics of our time. His deep understanding of the complexities of the "self," the unconscious, psychological types and archetypes took me on a deep journey of understanding my own psyche, and had I not taken this journey of knowing psyche and soma, which is the mind-body relationship, I don't believe I would have been as unafraid to face my soul, my shadow, and go deep into my unconscious through dream amplification and interpretation. I also feel that my burning desire to know more, and my own mystical experiences, helped lead me to those who have walked the path of spiritual and mystical awakening. Without these mystical trailblazers, I could not have lifted, or continue to lift, the veils of illusion that keep us believing we are separate, rather than a part of something greater which, as I've said throughout this book, has been called God, oneness, unity consciousness, or whatever a Divine presence means to you.

If we cannot recognize that this is what the mystical is; the spiritual mystery of life that keeps us in awe, fascination, and always wanting to know more, then we are not looking beyond just what we see, because, without question, there is so much more than what appears to the eye, and the mystic knows this. They are the brave ones, I feel, who go towards the invisible, and are unafraid to take those extra steps to be closer to the sacred truths of life. They are more comfortable with "who or what" comes to us when we pray. Not just when we need guidance, or ask for mercy, but knowing that we can communicate with a sacred, divine presence always, and know that it is listening. They can gently hold space for the spirit of a loved one who has left this earth and can speak to them as if they are still with us. The mystic can imbibe the soul of a tree, or intuit the soul of an animal. They can listen to the whispers of guardian angels, and are grateful for the messages from the etheric realms. The mystic doesn't think this is odd or strange. No, the mystic does not think that what is so easily interpreted as "esoteric" or "out there" or "other worldly" is odd or strange. We call these more spiritual or mystical experiences unusual, or even odd and strange, because we're afraid to accept that there is more than just us in our bodies, living a material existence that keeps us believing we'll never get old or die, which is what we fear the most. Those beliefs are not real. They are thoughts dictated by fear, and if you've experienced "eternal reality," as you can while having an oceanic experience (which Romain Rolland also described as "being one with the eternal world as whole"), then you know that the spirit continues on once it has left the body. It experiences not necessarily the "light at the end of the tunnel" but the light beyond the tunnel, as I like to say.

We must stop pretending that these altered states of consciousness are unnatural. We must stop perpetuating the belief that they are far too esoteric for most people to understand, and only those who have specialized knowledge understand it. That does not mean you can't understand it, too, but what is required of you is to regard mysticism as something that should be revered and handled with great care. If you begin with that, your relationship with mysticism can evolve naturally. Only you know where you would like to go with it. And where you will ultimately go with it is of your choosing, and yes, your understanding, or knowledge of it. You see, mysticism meets you where you are, and the person that is ready to meet it, will be greeted by it in the exact way they are ready to. You cannot go further than you are ready or prepared to go, and as the Chinese proverb goes, "Don't push the river, it flows by itself."

You just need to ask yourself if you are ready to be initiated into mysticism, and if so, why? What is it about mysticism that calls to you, because you need to be called to wanting to know more, and see more or go beyond the intellect and connect to something that many mystics have called the "ultimate reality." This "ultimate reality" can only be known by those who know it, and those who pretend they know, or use things like religion or spirituality to say they do, might not know it at all. They may use others who have known it, like Christ or Buddha, and tell you what they knew. How do they know what they knew? Yes, we have ancient wisdom that has been passed down through the ages, both orally, and in texts. But what I suggest is that you find out for yourself what the "sacred truths" are, and when you hear them preached, espoused, or pontificated on by others, see if what they say resonates with your understanding of the hidden, sacred truths. If it does, then those truths will pulsate in your soul, and "ultimate reality" will be known by those who know it.

I do think there's an element of privacy that needs to be kept and preserved around one's understanding of mysticism before it can be leaked, or shared with others. Mysticism is like fine wine that gets better with time.

There is a gestation period you must go through with it, and this can take months, years, or for all we know, life-times. The mystical path is ongoing, and isn't intended for dabbling. Instead, it is to be immersed in with all of your being. So, before you go ahead and call yourself a mystic, I suggest you follow some of the steps of initiation. One of those steps is similar to that of a "Mikveh," which is a Hebrew word for a bath used for "the purpose of ritual immersion in Judaism to achieve purity." According to the Torah laws, it requires a Jewish woman to dip into the Mikveh before she engages in marital relations. This is an ancient practice that "honors the sacred nature of our bodies." It is not only meant for women, but something that men can partake in too.

I'm going to take you into a purification ritual, but re-move the religious aspect from it, meaning it doesn't need to be only thought of as a Jewish ritual, nor do you have to be Jewish to do it. This is a purification of your soul, so that you can be ready to call in something as sacred as mysticism, which is very powerful, and you need to be pure of mind, body, and spirit. In essence, your mind can only be "lit up" if your thoughts are illumined. There is no other way for it to happen if it is true, divine illumination.

Do not get into this bath of purification I am about to guide you in unless you have made a concerted effort in keeping your thoughts illumined. I'm not saying that every single thought in our minds are filled with spiritual

light all the time. We may be heading towards enlightenment, but aren't quite there yet. But, if you practice Mindfulness with consistency, which is my criteria for engaging
in mysticism, you are aware of the thoughts you hold in
your mind, and very conscious of the ones that are "filled
with light" versus those that are not. Practicing thought
illumination means you know exactly what to do when a
thought comes up that wants to "disrupt a conscious state
of illumination," as I explained. Thoughts of fear or doubt
can create mental disruption, but you can change them
in an instant from negative to positive, if you choose to.
Remember what I said: 'we have a choice to always stay in
the 'light of our existence.'"

Please do not engage in mysticism if you are attached
to a particular story or narrative as to why negative
thoughts should be allowed for in your mind. If you have
a need to explore them, entertain them, or allow for them
to inhabit your mind, then spend as much time as you
need to understand the purpose of your negative thoughts
before you engage in mysticism. Negative thoughts may
be considered "normal," and we may be "predisposed" to
think negatively, as well as positively, but for many people,
their attachment to their negative thoughts goes beyond
merely a "disposition" we may have to think negatively on
occasion. Buried in their negative thoughts is a deeper
reason for why they are there, which is important to know.

As I say in my first book, Says Who?, "Know all of
your thoughts, not just the pretty ones." I also said that

"our thoughts have something important to tell us, or teach us, so it's necessary to delve deeper into them to find out what that is." I'm saying all of this because I want to make sure that you're doing the necessary psycho-spiritual work on yourself before you rush into mysticism, or are eager to have mystical experiences. Yes, the mystical experience can be blissful, euphoric, and even orgasmic, but this isn't sex we're talking about. This is a profound, transformational path to be on and let me be clear: it isn't always euphoric or orgasmic.

The mystical path can bring you to your knees in pain, humility, begging for forgiveness, or pleading for guidance when your soul feels so lost your despair tricks you into believing that you should die. The mystical path can have many dark nights, so I caution you against thinking this is only a journey of constant spiritual orgasms. Yes, experiencing a spiritual union can produce an altered state of consciousness, which can feel like a boundless state where orgasmic waves of energy can move through your entire being, but just like many people have experienced darkness, despair, inner demons, or pure hell on psychedelic drugs like LSD or Ayahuasca, you have to meet yourself where you are, and where you are is where you need to be. Nothing, not even the mystical experience, can change that unless you are ready for a spiritual transformation, and you will realize it when you are ready to.

Nothing outside of ourselves can do the spiritual work for us, meaning not a person, drugs, alcohol, or even mysticism. We must do the work, and when we are ready to be met with what can help us in our spiritual transformation, we will seek it out. It will take us into its embrace when we are prepared to be "energized by the invisible," as Evelyn Underhill described her mystical experience, or "become one with the spirit power of life itself," as Jane Goodall described feeling in hers.

Let me guide you in this purification ritual, and again, do it only if you feel truly ready to remove the obstacles, hindrances, stories, or narratives that keep you stuck in a less pure state of mind. This ritual is intended for you to gain more spiritual insights, but only if you are ready, will you realize them. I cannot overemphasize how important it is to keep your thoughts illumined as much as you can, and not wait for your thoughts to be magically illumined by immersing yourself in a spiritual cleansing. No short cuts here!

Let us begin:

1. Find a body of water into which you can immerse yourself.
2. This can be a bath, or you can do this out in nature, like in a lake or ocean.
3. Make sure that you have removed any jewelry, nail polish, and make-up if you want to do this like a traditional Jewish Mikveh, and especially remove all of your clothes before going into the water. If being fully

naked is not an option if you're out in public, try and wear a white bathing suit, trunks, or a tunic.

4. In a traditional Mikveh, there are seven steps to walk before entering the body of water for the ritual, which represents the "seven days of creation." Take seven steps towards the body of water in which you will be doing this ritual in, and think of seven as the number for mysticism, intuition, inner wisdom, and deep inner knowing, as it is thought of in numerology. Seven is regarded as a highly spiritual number. It is considered to be a great power number in Judaism, representing completeness and perfection. In your purification, you are preparing yourself for completeness and perfection, which is something we continue to do throughout our lifetime. I explained how we are in a constant state of "being and becoming" in Chapter 8, which means we are always in transition and transformation. It is said that those involved in the study of Jewish mysticism go to the Mikveh on a regular basis, and frequent immersions in it is essential for attaining the type of spiritual insights needed for transformation. You can do this ritual whenever you feel you want to experience a type of purification and receive the spiritual insights you need.

5. Close your eyes. Before you begin the ritual, think of what brought you here, and what you hope to leave behind in these waters. Setting your intentions is important so that you can be clear about why you're

doing this, what you hope to get from it, and what you intend to do with it moving forward. Take a few deep breaths in and out. Immerse your entire body, including your face under water three times. Either sit up or stand in the body of water you are in, and say silently, "Blessed are you, Majestic Spirit of the universe, who purifies me and makes me holy by embracing me in living waters." (You can replace "Majestic Spirit" with God, or whatever represents a Divine presence to you, such as: Hashem, Yahweh, Christ, Buddha, Krishna, Vishnu, Allah, Aya, supreme being, source, divine light, the eternal one, etc. This is not a religious ritual but a spiritual one, and if addressing a religious figure does not resonate for you, then direct this blessing to whomever, or whatever, you wish to, even if it's the sky, sun, moon, stars, or body of water you are in. Remember all things are sacred). And, if you want to create, or say your own blessings or prayers, you can, and even sing between immersions. This is your personal ritual, which can be whatever you want it to be. Invoke the sacred in your own way, but to get the most out of this ritual, you need to be open and available to the "invisible," meaning that which you can connect to, and be in "union" with your soul and the soul of he, she, it, or even nothing. There is sacredness even in emptiness, and if you view that which is sacred as being pure energy, then even God can be thought of as "pure spirit." This is what the "invisible" means; that which we cannot see, but trust that its presence is there.

6. Dunk, or immerse, your entire being in water again. Either sit up or stand in the body of water you are in, and say silently, "Blessed are you, Majestic Spirit of the Universe (fill in what you want) who has kept me alive, sustained me, and enabled me to reach this day." Again, this can be your own blessing, prayer, or song.

7. Dunk, or immerse your entire being in water again. Either sit up or stand in the body of water you are in, and say silently, "Blessed are you, Majestic Spirit of the Universe (fill in what you prefer, and again, this can be your own blessing, prayer or song). Thank you for sanctifying me in this sacred immersion and preparing me to receive the insights I need for my spiritual transformation. I will use these insights I receive wisely, and continue to receive for the raising of consciousness and the betterment of all."

8. Dunk, or immerse your entire being in water again. Either sit up or stand in the body of water you are in. Say a silent prayer to yourself. Take a few minutes to think about what you want to leave behind in the water and what you wish to take with you. Take as much time as you need in the water after the ritual is complete. This is a lovely opportunity to be with yourself in silence and feel the sacred energy that is moving in you, through you, and around you. You may be

aware of any insights you've gotten in this ritual either immediately, or it might come to you later in a dream, or even days later. You've opened yourself up to receive spiritual insights or messages, and they will come to you when you are ready to receive them.

This ritual is like a spiritual initiation, and it can have a significant effect on you. It can alter your life profoundly and change your thinking and perceptions in a whole new way. You may find that from the minute you sit quietly after the ritual, you not only feel differently, but when you look around you, it's as if you're seeing everything differently, more vibrant and more multidimensional, as I spoke about in Chapter 21 - Mystical Perception. Perhaps it's what Underhill calls, "achieving consciousness of a world that was always there." Now, after a spiritual initiation, you see what was there, but with an altered, "mystical perception." This perception is only perceivable when there has been a shift in consciousness, and this shift is necessary for the spiritual initiate. As Dion Fortune says in her quote above, "We take spiritual initiation when we become conscious of the Divine within us, and thereby contact the Divine without us."

As a spiritual initiate, he who sets his/herself on the path of mysticism, you must "become conscious of the Divine within you" as Dion Fortune says, before you can "contact the Divine without you," and now is the time to ask yourself the following: "Am I conscious of the Divine

within me?" If you have answered "yes," I say, "Welcome
to the path of mysticism!" You have entered the realm of
Divine Consciousness where you are all things, and all
things are you. There is no longer a separation, or dualism,
between you and all that exists; and oneness, or unity consciousness is your natural state. You will begin to see the
limitless expansion of Divine Consciousness more and
more each day and feel a more expansive state of being
within you, and without you. This means you can connect
to, or contact, the divine when you wish to. When you
do, what will you ask for, or do with it? Ah, such is the
power of the mystical path. Be careful with this newfound
love you have asked for. It is quite sacred, and worthy
of awe and respect. What it asks of you is to regard it as
the Goddess Sophia, the embodiment of wisdom, and
treat the Divine as you would treat what could possibly
be the Holy of Holies. And what do you think that is?
The mystic must contemplate this more deeply to know
what a true manifestation of holy is, especially in the 21st
Century.

Get ready to contemplate more, dear mystic. This is a
path of never-ending seeking, questioning, and contem-
plating.

Consider this quote by philosopher and mystic,
Meister Eckhart:

> *"What a man takes in by contemplation,*
> *that he pours out in love."*

I am a spiritual initiate
And have embarked on the
Mystical path
I have been invited
Into the inner sanctuary
Of the Divine
And must keep my mind
Illumined

Hidden truths
Are in the vault
Of this heavenly temple
Which I am blessed
To have entered
And perhaps
Come to know

CHAPTER 32

THE ILLUMINATED SOUL

Look at how a single candle can both defy
and define the darkness.

— ANNE FRANK

Perhaps a feature of the crucified face lurks in every mirror;
perhaps the face died, was erased, so that God may be all of us.
Who knows but that tonight we may see it in the labyrinth of
dreams, and tomorrow not know we saw it.

— JORGE LUIS BORGES

Even the sun directs our gaze away from itself
and to the life illumined by it.

— EBERHARD ARNOLD

Perhaps you might be thinking, "My soul is illuminated, now what?" What happens now is what you choose to do with your illuminated soul, which means you don't really need to do anything, but to allow your illuminated soul to lead the way in all that you do.

It is in both your "being and becoming" that your soul brightens even more, and if you think of yourself as "made of stardust," as Carl Sagan said we are, then you will light up the darkness everywhere you go. Those who are in your presence will feel your light, be touched by your light, and remember their own light if they have lost their way from it, or live more in darkness than light.

The mystic knows that this is the work of illumination, and there is nothing to be gained on the path of mysticism other than learning how to face darkness with light, overcome darkness with light, and lift the veils of illusion that try to darken the light by keeping sacred truths hidden. But the illuminated soul knows how to uncover these hidden truths, and only a soul that is truly illuminated can know the truths that are hidden.

Your job is to keep your soul illuminated, and when it gets hard to do, that is when you must dig deeper into your soul, and find whatever light is there even if your internal flame is low or feels weak. We cannot stay in the euphoria of mysticism at all times, and as I said, this is not a path of constant bliss. At times, your light will be challenged, and when you are facing your own darkness; a type of darkness that has you thinking it might not end, it is then that you must plunge into the depths of your being and remember that you are fierce like Joan of Arc was when she chose to listen to the voices that she claimed were angels and saints "through whom God was addressing her." It is said that the first of these voices spoke to her from her father's garden when she was thirteen, and when she heard them, it was accompanied by "a blinding white light." She feared them at first, but it is also said that she came to terms with the voices she continued to hear in her head, and she was even able to "beckon them at will."

And that's what the mystic can do. Beckon, or call forward, the help that is needed to keep its soul illuminated. As we know, the life journey has many challenges, and we cannot do this alone. We needn't believe that we are alone on this path of illumination. As I said, the sacred is all around us, we just need to believe it's there. Even if at times it is hard to believe in, or trust what is invisible; this "union with reality" that many mystics spoke about can test our faith to see if we believe in what we may not see, but know is there with every fiber of our being. As Evelyn Underhill said, "we are, in fact, being energized by what we cannot see, but know deep in our hearts is most real and true."

One of the hardest parts of being a mystic, or choosing the path of mysticism, is to find the path of illumination too demanding of our trust and faith in it, and you might find yourself wanting to reduce, or even quit your pursuit of the sacred. That is when you could entertain the possibility of living life as a mere mortal who doesn't need to know the hidden truths, whatever they might be.

No, we don't need to know the truths that are hidden, and maybe not knowing them keeps us in a more blissful state because, as the saying goes, "Ignorance is bliss." But is it? Is a lack of knowledge a good thing? Are we happier not knowing the truth? And if so, what truth are we choosing not to know to keep us happy, or happier than we would be if we knew it? I think that ignorance is actually a dangerous thing, and choosing "not to know" is a type of collusion with pretending, because it is convenient for us to not know something that is crucial for us to know.

Choosing to look away when darkness or evil is right in front of you, is choosing to collude with it, and that collusion is the very thing upon which evil feeds on; the very thing that keeps it alive. And that is when we feel misled. When some type of darkness or evil is upon us, but it is us who has allowed ourselves to be misled by it because we chose, or preferred not to see it.

As Leonardo da Vinci says, "Blinding ignorance does mislead us. O! Wretched mortals, open your eyes!" Open our eyes we must, and the true mystic knows this. Again, they are the brave souls who are unafraid to know the truth, as painful as that truth may be. Part of that truth is that evil exists as part of the nature of the universe but hidden in the deeper truths are the esoteric teachings and wisdom of why evil exists beyond the nature of the universe. Only the mystic who is advanced in their understanding of the cosmic plot and the purpose of creation can know it. This is why Talmudic scholars and Kabbalists, many of them mystics themselves, study the "wisdom of truth," and devote their lives to understanding these truths, which are considered esoteric, and aren't easy to understand. It is only those who have a burning desire to know more, or feel called to know, are the ones who can fully comprehend these ancient truths. By understanding them, they can explain these mystical teachings in a way that makes us think, ponder, and contemplate life, the universe, and our purpose here. If you're someone who wants to know, you will plunge deeper into the journey of knowing, and like the peeling of an onion, you will slowly peel the layers away so that you can know more. This is what the illuminated soul wishes to do.

I'm not saying that we are going to know everything there is to know. This is life school, my friends. It's hard to wrap your mind around how much there is to know. Consider something like The Dutch Ritman Library in Amsterdam, which recently added 20,000 books on philosophy, mysticism, religion, alchemy, astrology, and magic between 100 and 600 years old to its digital archives. Add to that the Talmudic Encyclopedia, which contains the world's largest electronic collection of Jewish texts in Hebrew ever recorded, embodying thousands of years of Jewish learning (Princeton University Library). Add to that the Gershom Sholem Library in the National Library of Israel, which specializes in the field of Kabbalah and Jewish Mysticism based on the personal library of Gershom Scholem, who was the renowned researcher of the Kabbalah. Well, clearly there is a whole hell of a lot to know!

Can we know everything? Let's just say we can know what we can know, and what we can know is entirely based on our capacity to know it. Most of us are not Kabbalists, or Talmudic scholars, but we certainly can study an area of ancient wisdom that interests us and learn much about it. Still, we can only know what we have the capacity to know. But, the mystic, who might not study just one particular thing, but many things that fall in the category of mysticism, can certainly come to know everything they can that is related to sacred knowledge, and it doesn't require you to be a scholar to know it. What it does require of you to be is an illuminated soul, which in and of itself is no easy thing to be. You see, there are certain requirements to know the secrets of the universe, and just because you think you should know them doesn't necessarily mean you will. Be careful of your ego pushing its way through when you want to covet knowledge that is sacred.

As we know, many people driven by ego, and even madness, took ancient wisdom, great mystery teachings, or divine guidance, and distorted it, or used it for their own selfish and greedy reasons and it backfired terribly. It is said that Aleister Crowley, who was an English occultist, and founded the religion Thelema, a "spiritual philosophy derived from Western esotericism," was called the "wickedest man in the world." He studied at Trinity College in Cambridge, and became a member of the Hermetic Order of the Golden Dawn, which was a secret society derived from the Rosicrucians, a "worldwide brotherhood claiming to possess esoteric wisdom handed down from ancient times."

The Order of the Golden Dawn was devoted to the study and practice of the occult, metaphysics, and paranormal activities during the late 19th century and early 20th centuries. Crowley, who apparently lived a very "decadent lifestyle," and had a talent for "creating controversy," was eventually forced out of the Order of the Golden Dawn. But that didn't stop him from continuing his life with little regard for "society's rules," which is when he founded his own religion. It is said that he began to hear voices, which supposedly was the spirit of the "Egyptian God Horus," and he wrote what were considered by his followers as "holy texts." Eventually the counterculture of the '60's and '70's embraced him, and he became a symbol of "rebellion and hidden wisdom." By others, he is considered satanic, and he has been called a "black magician."

It's interesting that the voices Crowley heard versus the voices that Joan of Arc heard were entirely different in what they instructed them to do. For Joan of Arc, her voices, which she claimed were the voices of "angels and saints" and "through whom God was addressing her," told her to help free her country from occupation. One voice in particular told her to "go to Orleans to break England's siege of France." She has been quoted as saying, "Whatever I have done that was good, I have done at the bidding of my voices." She believed she was receiving divine guidance from the voices she heard, and what she set out to do was considered saintly. Joan of Arc was canonized as a saint of the Roman Catholic Church on May 16, 1920 by Pope Benedict XV. Although she was burnt at the stake by "pro-English clergy" and called a witch, she subsequently became a "folk saint" among French Catholics and solders who believed she was being "commanded by God to fight for France against England."

Aleister Crowley, on the other hand, heard very different kinds of voices, and one in particular that "ordered him to steal the Egyptian Stele of Revealing," which is an Egyptian religious artifact in a museum in Cairo that dates back to the 26th dynasty. This artifact was very sacred to the Thelemites (an adherent of Thelema, Crowley's religion). Through it, Crowley received the mystical communication known as "The book of the Law" (also

known as Liber Al vel Legis), the sacred text of Thelema,
which were channeled verses.

Both Joan of Arc and Aleister Crowley heard voices
that came from somewhere that was considered a mystical guidance of some type. And both of them chose very
different paths for what moved their souls: Joan of Arc
clearly guided by light that only Archangel Michael could
be thought of as possessing, and whom she felt spoke to
her, too, and Crowley, who was driven by something many
think of as dark forces that ended up possessing him, and
causing him to continue his licentious lifestyle, and de-
scent into darkness. Perhaps he lived by his dictum, "Do
what thou wilt." He did exactly that in a way that pushed
the boundaries of light, and apparently darkness overcame
him.

Joan of Arc is considered a saint, and Crowley was
considered by many a sinner, or even worse, satanic.
These are two people who were guided by some form of
mysticism, and what one does with the path of sacred
knowledge, or divine guidance, is completely up to them.
As I said, it takes work to keep our souls illuminated, and
there are times when we may stumble, or even fall from
grace, because of our turning away from God's light. If
you wish not to think of this heavenly light coming from
an entity called God, then it is turning away from Divine
light, or whatever you want to call an invisible energy
source that doesn't need a name, but must be acknowl-

edged that it exists, and is, indeed, sacred. When we turn from it, we risk the dimming of our soul's illumination because we don't believe there is something greater than us that shines its light upon us, and we can draw from it to increase our own. Perhaps this is a type of cosmic energy, which is thought to be a "vital source that animates all forms of life and maintains the balance of the entire cosmos" according to ancient Sanskrit literature such as the Upanishads and Vedas. I'm good with that, and yet our ego can try to take full credit for our existence, and the existence of the universe and the cosmos.

We may be powerful, but that does not mean we are omnipotent, or all-knowing to the exclusion of a transcendent union we can choose to be in that is invisible, but again, must trust that it is there. Is there an "other" or "holy other?" If so, is this "other" separate from us? The state of oneness tells us this isn't so, therefore, we are at one with this light, energy, source, frequency, vibration, or whatever you want to call it, religious or not. Let's not get caught up in names or labels, and let's not also let our egos run the show here. If we don't manage and control our personal egos, as well as the "collective ego," which Eckhart Tolle describes in his book, A New Earth as manifesting "the same characteristics as the personal ego, such as the need for conflict and enemies, the need for more, the need to be right against others who are wrong, and so on," our egos will most definitely run the show. It seems in many ways they are by the chaos and conflicts we are witnessing all over the planet today.

I believe we are shined on by a divine source of light, and that we can draw light from this source whenever we want to, or need to especially when we're too ego driven, or embroiled in conflict, and we ourselves do not know how to free ourselves from it. This is why we have enemies and perpetuate what I call "enemy consciousness." This is another level of consciousness I'd like to add to the many states of consciousness, and consider this type of consciousness the impetus for wars. To quote Leonardo da Vinci again: "Blinding ignorance does mislead us. O! Wretched mortals, open your eyes!"

And open our eyes we must. We must recognize this divine source of light and understand that this divine radiance wants nothing more than for us to keep our souls illuminated so that we may continue to be "at one" with this divine radiance, and brighten this world more each day by our presence here.

Yes, we are made of "stardust," and as J.R.R. Tolkein says, "Moonlight drowns out all but the brightest stars."

I am an illuminated soul

Who seeks to know

Hidden truths

And sacred knowledge

I know it can only

Be revealed to me

When I keep my soul illuminated

If I turn away from

Divine light

Truths become hidden

Sacred knowledge

Beyond my grasp

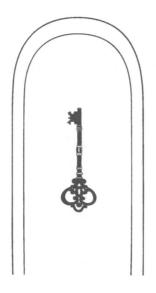

MINDFULNESS & MYSTICISM

CHAPTER 33

MYSTERIUM TREMENDUM
(ET FASCINANS)

*Down below the broad, roaring waves of the sea break against
the deep foundation of the rock. But high above the mountain,
the sea, and the peaks of rock the eternal ornamentation
blooms silently from the dark depths of the universe.*

— RUDOLF OTTO

*God is the "mysterium tremendum," that appears and
overthrows, but he is also the mystery of the self-evident,
nearer to me than my I.*

— MARTIN BUBER

*It is not so much the things we know that terrify us as it is the
things we do not know, the things that break all known laws
and rules, the things that come upon us unaware and shatter
the pleasant dream of our little world.*

— DONALD WANDREI

The expression, "mysterium tremendum," which translates as "great mystery" or "awe-inspiring mystery," and "et fascinans" as "fascinating," is a Latin phrase that was introduced by German theologian and philosopher, Rudolf Otto. He was known for his investigation of "man's experience of the holy," and is considered to be one of the most influential scholars of religion. He is best known for coining the term, "numinous," which means a profound emotional experience that can "arouse spiritual or religious emotion," when one feels the power, presence, or has a realization of a divinity; a supernatural power such as God, supreme being, source, creator, or anything that is regarded as sacred and holy.

I've written extensively throughout this book on the mystical experience, which has been called "union with a transcendent reality," and how this union can be awe-inspiring. But the mystical can also be frightening as well as fascinating, and for many, they are repelled by the idea of there being something mysterious about this life. They choose to steer away from it, or might not even hold the idea that there is anything mysterious about this life, the universe, the cosmos, and even us. Quite simply, there is nothing more to know.

I can understand how the invisible spiritual world can be awe-inspiring to those who have felt it, or experienced it, and frightening to those who have not. For the mystic, it feels natural to accept the hidden world of the divine, meaning what is invisible, and it is the very thing that cannot be seen, yet felt, that the mystic welcomes, or goes in search of. When they know they are in the presence of it, they are not in doubt of it, or fear it, because for them it feels very real, and yes, numinous.

In Otto's influential book, Das Heilige, which was translated in English to The Idea of the Holy, he writes the following:

"The feeling of it may at times come sweeping like a gentle tide pervading the mind with a tranquil mood of deepest worship. It may pass over into a more set and lasting attitude of the soul, continuing, as it were, thrillingly vibrant and resonant, until, at last, it dies away and the soul resumes its 'profane,' non-religious mood of everyday experience. It has its crude, barbaric antecedents and early manifestations, and again it may be developed into something beautiful and pure and glorious. It may become the hushed, trembling, and speechless humility of the creature in the presence of—whom or what? In the presence of that which is a Mystery inexpressible and above all creatures."

We may not know the "whom or what" we are in the "presence of," but why can't this be okay? Can't we trust that this feeling which can "come sweeping like a gentle tide pervading the mind with a tranquil mood of deepest worship," is so "thrillingly vibrant and resonant" that we don't want it to die away? And it doesn't have to. This "vibrant and resonant" feeling can be with us always, and when we get taken or pulled away from it by our everyday, routine, and at times, mundane life, we are eager to return to it because we know that this great mystery, mysterium tremendum is "inexpressible and above all creatures," and yes, it can be "developed into something beautiful and pure and glorious."

Do not fear that which you cannot see, but instead, ask to see it. Ask the "whom" or the "what" you feel you might be in the presence of to show itself to you, and you will be shown it. But not if you don't believe that you are in the presence of the numinous. No, you will not be shown anything if you don't believe that the numinous is real. Accept this supernatural power that exists, and if you cannot, ask yourself why not. You are not being asked to believe in religion, or God, or to worship this supernatural power. That is what man has created for the explanation of the divine because he feels that the divine needs to be explained religiously, and for many that is the only way it makes sense or can be believable. It's as if the invisible must be made visible, or else it does not, or cannot exist. Stop insisting that the invisible be made visible, and begin to trust more of what Rudolf Otto described as "inexpressible and above all creatures." This is the great mystery, and yes, it exists. It might inspire awe in you, or it might make you tremble, but even if it does "provoke terror" in you, as Otto said it could, and can, as he also said "present itself as overwhelming power," again, do not fear it.

This great mystery, mysterium tremendum can "come sweeping like a gentle tide pervading the mind with a tranquil mood" as Otto describes it so beautifully, if you let it. But it cannot come to you if you resist it, or don't believe it is possible. The numinous is "wholly other," as Otto described it, and it is "entirely different from anything we experience in ordinary life." I asked you early on if you wanted to live a more divine life, or do you prefer it to be ordinary? What is it that you want? Do you know? What calls to you in the depths of your being? Would you like to experience this great mystery, mysterium tremendum? You can.

Let me guide you in a meditation to call in the great mystery:

1. Find a quiet place to sit.
2. Close your eyes.
3. Take a few deep breaths in and out.
4. Sit with the silence.
5. Observe yourself sitting in silence.
6. Be aware of any thoughts, feelings, or bodily sensations. Simply observe them.
7. Recognize that you are more than your body.
8. Acknowledge your spirit within the vehicle of your body.
9. Feel your spirit permeate beyond your body.

10. Feel the energy of your spirit around you.

11. Imagine the energy of your spirit connect to an all-pervading power beyond the energy of your spirit.

12. Imagine it as an all-pervading power that is infinite.

13. Imagine that you are now a part of this all-pervading power.

14. Sense what you cannot see.

15. Feel what you cannot see.

16. Touch what you cannot see.

17. Trust what you cannot see.

18. Say silently, "An all-pervading power has me in its embrace."

19. Say silently, "This all-pervading power is the great mystery."

20. Say silently, "I have entered the great mystery."

21. Say silently, "The great mystery has entered me."

22. Spend as much time as you can with it. This is meant to penetrate you deeply, and it can be a profound, life altering experience. Whatever it is, accept it with non-judgment, and trust that whatever you experienced is what you are meant to know and understand at this time.

23. When you are ready slowly open your eyes.

24. Take as much time as you need to transition out of your meditation.

The great mystery wants to be known, not feared. It wants us to know it the way God wants us to know him/her, and the universe wants us to know it, and the cosmos wants us to know it, and the sun wants us to know it, and the moon wants us to know it. They are here with us. They exist as we exist. Why would we choose to deny their presence, or make them feel they are not important, or precious, or sacred? That's like saying we aren't important, or precious, or sacred. Are we not? What vacuum do we think we are supposed to live in? If you don't think there is mystery to this life, then you are eons away from the great mystery, Mysterium Tremendum. But the truth is that "every mystery of life has its origin in the heart," as priest and theologian Hans Urs von Balthasar described it.

Yes, these mysteries of life begin in our hearts, and the mystic knows this. That is why some mystics describe their union with the great mystery as a love between them and their Divine Beloved, which I will go into more in the next chapter. They feel that they are taken into an ecstatic state of consciousness, and it is the love they have in their hearts for the sacred that allows for that to happen. You cannot be taken, or seduced into the great mystery unless you want to. It is your desire to be coupled with the "Absolute," or "the sum of all being," as German philosopher Hegel called it, and which can also be called "oneness" to which you open your heart to. Many mystics have felt pure ecstasy when they allowed themselves to be enraptured in the divine.

The great mystery awaits us. It asks to come towards it. It does not want us to fear it, and if we tremble, it should be because we are in the presence of something that wants us to realize something sacred about ourselves and that is, we are not separate from it. The great mystery is a part of us, our soul, and it is what keeps it illuminated.

I have been taken into

The Great Mystery

Oh Mysterium Tremendum

You have allowed me to know you

And even when I doubted you

Or feared you

You never turned away

You waited for me in silence

Until I was ready

And showed yourself to me

Filling me with ecstasy

MINDFULNESS & MYSTICISM

LOVER AND DIVINE BELOVED

The way the Beloved can fit in my heart, two thousand lives could fit in this body of mine. One kernel could contain a thousand bushels, and a hundred worlds pass through the eye of the needle.

— RUMI

Love abounds in all things, excels from the depths to beyond the stars, is lovingly disposed to all things.

— HILDEGARD OF BINGEN

Deep within the heart of a true mystic, you will find profound love for the divine, and this mystical relationship is one of Lover and Divine Beloved, which I mentioned previously. It is quite a different type of love than that between two embodied people because the mystical relationship of Lover and Divine Beloved is a type of love that "abounds in all things," as mystic Hildegard of Bingen said, and "excels from the depths to beyond the stars." Not that corporeal love can't take you "beyond the stars." But the type of love I'd like to focus on is the mystical relationship of Lover and Divine Beloved, which is not just the love for one person, but love for all of creation.

When one embarks on the mystical journey, one is having a love affair with the numinous, which I spoke about in the previous chapter, Mysterium Tremendum. And, the numinous, as was described by Rudolf Otto, is a profound emotional experience, or "arouses spiritual or religious emotion" when one feels the power, presence, or has a realization of a divinity, a supernatural power such as God, supreme being, source, creator, or anything that is regarded as sacred and holy.

For the mystic, there is a constant opening and unfolding of this love affair, and they can feel as if it is a never-ending love that goes beyond time and space, which is how oneness is described. It's as if when we experience this feeling of wholeness, non-duality, and completeness, time stands still, and everything in the universe is aligned with eternal intelligence. We may think of this state of consciousness as impossible to sustain, and it may be, as it is very challenging to avoid daily interferences and distractions. But in the same way we are inclined to protect the love we have for another, and not allow for the spoiling of it by external factors, the mystic knows that their relationship to the Divine Beloved transcends disturbances. Much like one who is spiritual or religious can feel when entering a holy place like a temple, church, or mosque; this is where disturbance does not enter because the numinous is present, and nothing can interfere with its holiness.

There is a type of impenetrability to the relationship between the Lover and Divine Beloved that cannot be pierced, and which remains pure and protected. What this means is we do not allow for the tainting or besmirching of what is divine, holy, or sacred, which has been one of man's greatest challenges and could be called "falling from grace." When we lose respect for what is divine and sacred, and feel we can turn our back on it; pretty much doing whatever we damn well please, then yes, we run the risk of spoiling and tarnishing what is sacred like our planet, for example, and that is when we "fall."

I prefer taking this idiom, "To fall from grace" out of a biblical context, and put it in everyday life, and how we fall time and time again from spiritual consciousness, which the mystic is committed to developing in them-

selves. Do we "fall from grace" because of our "disobedience to God," as the Bible says? I think we fall from grace
because of our disobedience to the sacred. Again, if that's
God, a Divine presence or being, or something or someone with no name, and you have acted disrespectfully, and
done things that have shown or proven your disrespect
such as hurting others, or allowing for your mind not to
be illumined, or your heart to be filled with hate or preju-
dice instead of love, or actively chosen not to preserve the
wellbeing of the planet, and deliberately turned your back
on the sacred and all of its many manifestations from human, to animal, to nature, then yes, you have fallen from
grace in some way. And haven't we all fallen to varying
degrees?

We must take our love higher, and for the mystic, they
know that each day their love must rise so that there is no
"falling from grace," for each time we allow ourselves to
fall, it is that much harder to pick ourselves up again. This
is how the mystic shows their respect for the sacred, by
constantly taking their love for the Divine Beloved higher,
even if their beloved cannot be seen, only profoundly felt.
They know that it is present, and always worthy of their
regard and respect. And when the Divine Beloved shows
them they are there by the miracles they present to them,
they are awe-struck time and time again.

To embark on the mystical path, one must know for
certain that this is where their love belongs, and they

continue to rise as a human being to meet the sacred. All
of creation is divine, holy, and sacred, and as mystic Hildegard of Bingen says in her quote above, "Love abounds
in all things, excels from the depths to beyond the stars, is
lovingly disposed to all things."

So, we must ask ourselves the following: "How respectfully do I love?" meaning in what ways do I show
my love with honor and respect, whether it be my love
for another, or a "holy other"? And then we ask, "How is
my love sacred?" and "How do I keep my love sacred so it
doesn't vacillate, wane, or become spoiled or tarnished?"
When we love another, we rely on that love to sustain
us. As I said in Chapter 18 - Ascending Through Contemplation, "our love (for another) can diminish with
time because we expect love to keep taking us to greater
heights." Yes, love can certainly take us to great heights,
but I also said that "we will be dropped from its elevation
if we don't meet it with a greater love we must realize on
our own, and this love is 'transcendent' and 'abundant,'
which we must bring to every moment of our life to stay
in a heightened state of awareness, and continue to raise
our consciousness."

And that is what divine love teaches us. It teaches us
to love something greater than ourselves, and trust that
we can look to it for guidance and wisdom so that we
can expand our capacity to love beyond what we rely on
to satisfy or sustain us. We are so used to the love we get

from others to keep us feeling deserving and worthy, and when that love is no longer given to us, we feel we have failed somehow as a human being. This is when we can feel that God doesn't love us, for He does not shine His light or love upon us.

What comes to mind are the words of Christ: "My God, my God, why have you forsaken me?" This passage, which has been said Christ uttered when he was on the cross, is considered "difficult" to interpret, and can mean many things depending on who is interpreting it. According to the gospel writer Matthew (Matthew 27:46), he does not give a reason for Christ's "cry of dereliction," a feeling of God's abandonment of him, but much of what's been written about these words, and been repeated from the Bible by many priests and preachers over the ages, is that it speaks more about the "spiritual agony of Christ" rather than the physical suffering He endured.

As I've said many times about this book, it is not meant to be religious; therefore, I won't spend time on giving religious explanations, especially when it comes to the sacred words of Christ. But I'd like to weigh in on them in a way that resonates in my soul. Asking God why He has forsaken us, to me, means that we are asking God why He has turned his back on us. And haven't we felt that at certain times in our lives? We ask that God (or a Divine being or presence) answer our prayers when we speak to Him, and for some people they feel that their prayers are answered. But it is when we don't feel that God (or a Divine being or presence) has answered what we ask of Him (or Her if you feel that God is a woman) that we question the existence of God (or a Divine being or presence). That is when we can lose our belief or trust in something or someone we hold as Divine or sacred. It is when we are not given the love we need that we can not only doubt our worthiness of it, but we can also regard a divine love as something not worthy of us working so hard to get.

But, if we feel that love "abounds in all things, excels from the depths to beyond the stars, and is lovingly disposed to all things," as Hildegard of Bingen felt that it did, then we do believe that it is always present and in all things. And if, or when, we don't feel its presence, and perhaps doubt that it exists, we choose not to turn our back on it, rather than thinking it has turned its back on us. We remain steadfast in our love for the Divine Beloved.

Is it hard to trust that divine love is there for us always? Absolutely! Especially when we are suffering. "My God, my God, why have you forsaken me," has also been interpreted as it was Christ "fighting for humanity" or "our sins that he died for," if you subscribe to the Christian interpretation of it.

Who are we fighting for? Are we not fighting for the love we need to give ourselves? The love of which we feel we are so deserving? If we cannot ask ourselves questions like that, or probe the depths of our being so that we can know exactly how respectfully do we love, and how committed we are to the love we have, be it for another person, or a "holy other," than we don't really know what our capacity for a more divine love is.

Divine love lives within us, and we have the capacity to give and project this divine love outward. If we wait for it to be given to us, then we are always in waiting for a love greater than we can imagine. Can only the mystic know this love of lover and Divine Beloved? Those that are in "union with reality" can know it, and what we know of this transcendent reality is that it is filled with all that is sacred.

And what is sacred? All that exists.

Oh my ~~Divine Beloved~~

You have taught me how to love

~~Beyond the capacity I thought~~

I possessed

In darkness

Pain

And even doubt

You remained
Close to me
Never turning away
Even when I had
Turned away from you
And when I returned
You were there
For you never once left me

CHAPTER 35

ENTERING THE MYSTERY

*How great is the mystery of the first cells which were one
day animated by the breath of our souls! How impossible to
decipher the welding of successive influences in which we are
forever incorporated! In each one of us, through matter, the
whole history of the world is in part reflected.*

— PIERRE TEILHARD DE CHARDIN

The greatest mystery of existence is existence itself.

— DEEPAK CHOPRA

*The Creator, in taking infinite pains to shroud with mystery
His presence in every atom of creation, could have had but one
motive - a sensitive desire that men seek Him only through
free will.*

— PARAMAHANSA YOGANANDA

*We think we have solved the mystery of creation. Maybe we
should patent the universe and charge everyone royalties for
their existence.*

— STEPHEN HAWKING

You are now in the mystery. You have entered into its greatness. You have witnessed the numinous. You have stood in awe, and perhaps trembled in the presence of Mysterium Tremendum. You have declared love to the Divine Beloved, and now you exist in the knowing that there is something greater than you, something sacred that is always there, even if you cannot see it.

You will now live knowing that you exist in the mystery, and that the mystery is always there, in you, around you, everywhere. So, you will live your days knowing that life is a mystery, and you are in its embrace. This knowing has been bestowed upon you by the all-knowing creator of the mystery because you have chosen to know it, but it can easily be stopped if you choose to stop knowing.

The mystery is infinite. It never stops. It continues on, even when we no longer exist. We are visitors of the great mystery, and we live within it for a certain amount of time. What we choose to know while we are alive in the mystery is there for us to know. But if we don't respect the gifts it has to offer us, and choose instead to take it for granted, or misuse or abuse it, the mystery recedes back into the hidden depths of the universe, and this is where the sacred truths reside.

The mystic asks to know these hidden truths, and vows to respect and love the Divine Beloved knowing that the Divine Beloved is the mystery. They have joined the mystery in a spiritual marriage, and understand that they are "in union" with a reality that is transcendent. This union is protected and considered holy. They live each day honoring the holiness of this union, and in everything they do, and with everyone with whom they are in contact with, this holiness shines from their soul.

The mystic's journey is sublime, and it is also incredibly arduous. They know that suffering has helped them; prepared them to be ready to meet the great mystery, the Divine Beloved. Do not expect to live in the mystery if you resist suffering. You must know what pains your heart and ails your soul. You must be brave in the blackness of the dark night of the soul, and instead of wishing to die, you must beg to live, and to live with a greater knowing of why you are here in this life. Do not be fooled to think that the mystery will just be given to you. It will not. Yes, the mystery wants you to know it, but it cannot let itself be known to you if you are not ready, or not worthy of its knowing. Worthy, you might ask? How might you not be worthy?

You must ask yourself if you are. Where have you fallen instead of risen? When have you looked away from darkness or evil when you felt its presence, or saw it inflicted upon others? When have you allowed for your mind to be poisoned with thoughts that were not illumined, but instead permitted thoughts of greed, selfishness, envy, or even hate? When have you lied instead of spoken the truth? When have you fed your ego, letting it control you like a hungry tiger that demands you feed it? When have you not loved the great Mother Earth, or used her for your needs without honoring hers? When did you let fear make you cower, instead of being brave and heroic? And when did you turn your back on yourself? When did you declare yourself unworthy?

We have all been unworthy. We have all allowed ourselves to fall from grace, when instead we could have chosen to rise. But the mystery knows that this can happen, and the mystery gives us many signs to awaken from our unconsciousness. All that the mystery asks of us is to see these signs. But sometimes they are not so visible to us, which is why we have to look beyond the first layer of truth, and go much further in our seeing, so that we can see what is not so easy to see.

The mystery is ready for you. Are you ready for the mystery?

Let me guide you in a meditation where you can find out if you are.

1. Sit somewhere quiet.
2. Close your eyes.
3. Take a few deep breaths in and out.
4. Note any thoughts, feelings, or bodily sensations you might be feeling. Simply observe them.
5. Say silently, "I wish to enter the mystery."
6. Ask yourself silently, "Am I ready to enter the mystery?"

7. Answer silently either "yes" or "no."

8. If you answered "no," stop the meditation, and try this at another time when you feel ready.

9. If you answered "yes," continue.

10. Consider that you have entered into a holy place. You might think of it as a temple, church, or mosque.

11. See an image of it in your third eye, the space between your brow that I have guided you in before. Perhaps this holy place has stained glass windows, or is gothic or medieval, or maybe it's futuristic and made entirely of glass, and might even be on another planet. Whatever it is, keep creating it as you go deeper into seeing it.

12. Allow yourself to feel the numinous, the presence of divinity within the core of your being.

13. Ask to be taken deeper into this holy place you have created.

14. Imagine yourself there, and see it more clearly and vividly as you continue to create it in your mind.

15. Ask yourself silently, "Am I ready to know what is contained within this holy place?"

16. If you answered "no," stop the meditation.

17. If you answered "yes," continue.

18. Ask yourself silently, "What of the sacred truths can I know at this time?"

19. Listen silently to what you will hear.

20. If there is something that you hear, say silently,

"Thank you for revealing a sacred truth to me.
I know there are many more for me to know."

21. Say silently, "I am worthy of this sacred truth."

22. Say silently, "I will use this sacred truth for the raising of my consciousness, and the betterment of all."

23. Say silently, "I acknowledge this holy place as the container of sacred truths, and know that I must continue awakening my consciousness to know more."

24. Say silently, "I am committed to developing and strengthening my spiritual consciousness to know more."

25. Put your hands on your heart, and see yourself quietly walk out of this holy place.

26. When you are ready, open your eyes.

27. Sit in silence for as long as you can to be with what you experienced, and stay connected to what you feel. Do not rush to begin another activity. This meditation honors the sacred, and it is best if you remain silent for as long as you can. A cup of tea, a bath, or sitting under a tree is a lovely compliment for this meditation.

If you feel that you have entered the mystery, I smile and bow at your arrival. I know what you have realized in your heart to bring yourself here. You are a beautiful soul, and yes, you are worthy of the mystery. But now you must honor your arrival by keeping yourself present, aware, and committed to heightening your awareness, and raising your consciousness even more. Each day that you awaken, acknowledge the gift of your existence, and ask for guidance on the mystical path upon which you have embarked. Keep your mind illumined, and always remember to take your spiritual pulse so that you may gauge the needs of your soul. Darkness will visit you, as darkness does, but know that your light is far too radiant to fear it. You are the light in the darkness, and if anything, darkness should fear your light.

Continue to lift the veils of illusion, for there are many veils to lift on the mystical path. You will become an excellent veil lifter because you are committed to knowing the sacred truths, and you will know them with each veil that you lift. I admire your desire and courage to live the mystical life, and when you have visits of ecstasy, stop and allow it to "roll at your feet," as Kafka said. Also know, as he said, "you do not need to leave your room. Remain sitting at your table and listen. Do not even listen, simply wait, be quiet, still, and solitary."

You will know that the mystery is here, and that the mystery is you. By connecting to the Divine outside of you, you are now conscious of the Divine Mystery within you.

Ego Sum Mysterium

I am the Mystery

Ora Nadrich is a pioneering Mindfulness expert, international keynote speaker and coach, and the founder and president of the Institute for Transformational Thinking. Bestselling author Marianne Williamson has said, "When she speaks, I listen; when she writes, I read it; when she gives advice, I heed it." Ora is a sought-after expert in the fields of Mindfulness, transformational thinking, and self-discovery. Ora created and popularized her highly-effective "Says Who? Method" which allows her clients to ask simple questions that result in profound, personal and professional transformation. Ora is the author of "Says Who? How One Simple Question Can Change the Way You Think Forever", and "Live True: A Mindfulness Guide to Authenticity", named "one of the 100 Best Mindfulness Books of All Time" by BookAuthority, which is the world's leading site for book recommendations by thought leaders.

MINDFULNESS & MYSTICISM